SAGGER ANTI-TANK MISSILE
VS
M60 MAIN BATTLE TANK

Yom Kippur War 1973

CHRIS McNAB

Osprey Publishing
c/o Bloomsbury Publishing Plc
PO Box 883, Oxford, OX1 9PL, UK
Or
c/o Bloomsbury Publishing Inc.
1385 Broadway, 5th Floor, New York, NY 10018, USA
E-mail: info@ospreypublishing.com

www.ospreypublishing.com

OSPREY is a trademark of Osprey Publishing Ltd, a division of Bloomsbury
Publishing Plc.

First published in Great Britain in 2018

© 2018 Osprey Publishing Ltd

A CIP catalogue record for this book is available from the British Library.

ISBN: PB: 978 1 4728 2577 3
          ePub: 978 1 4728 2578 0
          ePDF: 978 1 4728 2579 7
          XML: 978 1 4728 2576 6

18 19 20 21 22   10 9 8 7 6 5 4 3 2 1

Index by Rob Munro
Typeset in ITC Conduit and Adobe Garamond
Map and tactical diagrams by bounford.com
Page layouts by PDQ Digital Media Solutions, Bungay, UK
Printed in China through World Print Ltd.

Osprey Publishing supports the Woodland Trust, the UK's leading woodland
conservation charity. Between 2014 and 2018 our donations are being spent
on their Centenary Woods project in the UK.

To find out more about our authors and books visit **www.ospreypublishing.
com**. Here you will find extracts, author interviews, details of forthcoming
events and the option to sign up for our newsletter.

Acknowledgements

As always, I would like to thank Nick Reynolds at Osprey for his help in
guiding this book through to publication. Thanks also go to Johnny Shumate,
for creating the excellent battlescene artworks, and also to Alan Gilliland for
the technical artworks, both of whose work helps to bring this study further to
life. Finally thanks go to Katie Thompson, of The Tank Museum, Bovington,
for her assistance in sourcing some of the complex technical information
surrounding this subject.

Excerpts from THE YOM KIPPUR WAR: THE EPIC ENCOUNTER
THAT TRANSFORMED THE MIDDLE EAST by Abraham Rabinovich,
copyright © 2004 by Abraham Rabinovich. Used by permission of Schocken
Books, an imprint of the Knopf Doubleday Publishing Group, a division of
Penguin Random House LLC. All rights reserved.

Excerpts from *The Egyptian Strategy for the Yom Kippur War: An Analysis* ©
2009 Dani Asher. Translated by Moshe Tlamim by permission of McFarland
& Company, Inc., Box 611, Jefferson NC 28640. www.mcfarlandpub.com

Title-page photograph: Sagger missile and control unit components on display.
The 9S415 joystick control unit on the right is minus the 9Sh16 periscope
sight. Note how the lid of the suitcase only forms the launch rail system,
although Saggers can be launched from the assembled suitcase with some
adjustments (typically sandbags around the base). (AirSeaLand Photos/Cody
Images)

Editor's note

With the exception of some weapons calibres, metric measurements are used
in this book. For ease of comparison please refer to the following conversion
table:

1km = 0.62 miles
1m = 1.09yd
1m = 3.28ft
1m = 39.37in
1cm = 0.39in
1mm = 0.04in
1kg = 2.20lb
1g = 0.04oz

Key to military symbols

Army Group	Army	Corps	Division	Brigade	Regiment	Battalion
Company/Battery	Platoon	Section	Squad	Infantry	Artillery	Cavalry
Airborne	Unit HQ	Air defence	Air Force	Air mobile	Air transportable	Amphibious
Anti-tank	Armour	Air aviation	Bridging	Engineer	Headquarters	Maintenance
Medical	Missile	Mountain	Navy	Nuclear, biological, chemical	Ordnance	Parachute
Reconnaissance	Signal	Supply	Transport movement	Fortress or static	Fortress machine gun	

Key to unit identification

Unit identifier — Parent unit
Commander
(+) with added elements
(−) less elements

CONTENTS

INTRODUCTION

The Yom Kippur War of 1973, also known as the 'October War', sits at a special juncture in Cold War history. From the perspective of our current age that, at least at the time of writing, is doctrinally dominated by light mobile warfare (counter-insurgency, rapid deployment, 'asymmetric' warfare, etc.), it is easy to forget the rather different priorities of conventional warfare in the 1960s and 1970s. The strategic and tactical thinking on both sides of the Iron Curtain was largely focused on the delivery of nuclear weapons and, on the ground, the movement of armoured forces. This was the age of the tank. The main battle tank (MBT), fighting in volume, was regarded as the metal fist of offensive warfare. In war colleges and training grounds around the world, military commanders spent much of their time thinking about how to use armour both to defeat the other side's tanks in open battle, and how to drive deep into enemy territory with armoured elements.

This was as true in the cauldron of the Middle East as in Central Europe. Since the establishment of the State of Israel in May 1948, and the new nation's immediate descent into conflict with its Arab neighbours, the Middle East had become a virtual test bed for the tactics and technologies of the Cold War. The open ground that characterized many of the battlefields, especially in the Sinai Desert, meant that tank-vs-tank combat was common and critical to the outcome of the clash. Israel and its chief opponents – Egypt, Syria, Jordan, Iraq, Saudi Arabia and Iran – therefore sank huge financial investment into purchasing armour in both quantity and quality. Israel typically went to the United States and the United Kingdom for its armour (and also utilized plentiful volumes of captured Arab kit), while the Arab nations shopped principally in the Eastern Bloc.

Yet in the Yom Kippur War, a new and shocking weapon disrupted the tactical picture of armoured warfare and resulted in what military historian Abraham

An AT-3 'Sagger' anti-tank guided missile (ATGM) in its classic 'suitcase' configuration. Note the red-tipped flare mounted between the two fins angled towards the viewer. This flare would ignite when the missile was launched, providing a visual tracking aid for the operator throughout the entire period of flight. (AirSeaLand Photos/Cody Images/MoserB)

Rabinovich has called the 'humbling of the tank' (Rabinovich 2004: 107). This was the deployment in mass of the early generations of anti-tank guided weapons (ATGWs), or anti-tank guided missiles (ATGMs), most prominently in the form of the 9M14 *Malyutka*, better known in the West by its NATO (North Atlantic Treaty Organization) codename, AT-3 'Sagger'. Rather like the disruption caused by the introduction of hand-held firearms in the medieval period, whereby an ill-trained footsoldier gained the personal firepower to unseat and kill a powerful knight, the two- or three-man Arab Sagger teams had the capability of killing any Israeli MBT. Anti-tank weapons were nothing new – World War II had seen plenty of tank-killing devices – but the introduction of Sagger batteries en masse, each missile able to destroy a tank out to a range of 3km, changed the nature of manoeuvre warfare in the Middle East.

If there is any doubt about the tactical shock unleashed by the advent of the Sagger missile and its ilk, just consider the 1975 report from the US Army's Training and Doctrine Command (TRADOC), entitled *Soviet ATGMs: Capabilities and Countermeasures*. The meat of the report is largely a sober analysis of the Yom Kippur War. Here the writers reflect upon how the world of armour had been changed by the conflict:

> All the modern armies of NATO, the Warsaw Pact, the Arab and Israeli nations generally
> agree that the main offensive weapon of ground forces is the tank. With its heavy
> armament, armor protection, and cross-country mobility, only the tank can break
> through an enemy force and engage or defeat it decisively. While the Arab-Israeli War of
> October 1973 (The "Yom Kippur War") reaffirmed the offensive potential of the tank,
> it has also dramatized the lethality of modern antitank weapons – particularly the high
> velocity tank cannon and the long-range antitank guided missile (ATGM). The effect of
> these modern antitank weapons in this war was devastating. Not since the Battle of Kursk

Israel Defense Forces (IDF) tank crews race to their M60 tanks during an exercise in the early 1970s. Note how some of the men carry the 9mm Uzi submachine gun; this was a popular weapon for tankers, as the compact firearm could be easily stowed inside an already crowded fighting compartment. (AirSeaLand Photos/Cody Images)

between the Germans and Russians in World War II has there been a comparable loss of tanks in such a short period of time. If the rate of loss which occurred in the Yom Kippur War during the short 20 days of battle were extrapolated to the European battlefields over a period of 60–90 days, the resulting losses would reach levels for which the United States Army is totally unprepared. While it is impossible to say precisely how many losses were attributable to a certain weapons system, we can say, particularly in view of the vast numbers of ATGMs employed, that the *antitank guided missile was responsible for a high percentage of the Israeli tank losses at the beginning of that war*. (US TRADOC 1975: 3)

There is almost a breathlessness in this writing, as if the authors are staring at the immense pile of doctrinal documents that need to be rewritten in light of the Sagger's influence. Furthermore, the Israelis were heavily reliant on US kit, not least the latest vehicle in their armoured inventory, the M60 and M60A1 Patton MBTs, known in Israeli service as the Magach 6 and Magach 6A respectively. This book filters out the many threads of the Yom Kippur War to focus on the clash between these two contrasting opponents. On the one hand, the M60/M60A1 tank with its heavy armour, powerful engine and far-reaching, accurate 105mm main gun. On the other, principally Egyptian Sagger ATGW teams, frail human beings made more powerful by a new and mobile anti-tank technology. What we shall see in this clash is the age-old battle between offence and defence, measure and countermeasure. We shall also see how the capabilities of individual weapons are not purely governed by their own intrinsic performance, but also by the tactical competency of the forces in which they serve. For while the Sagger missile might have brought about the 'humbling of the tank', such a reverse was only partial.

CHRONOLOGY

1961
July Development of the 9M14 *Malyutka* (AT-3 'Sagger') begins.

1963
16 September The 9M14 *Malyutka* is accepted for Soviet service, and soon begins selling to export clients.

1967
5–10 June Israel wins a stunning victory in the Six-Day War.
15 June The 'War of Attrition' begins, with fighting around the Suez Canal Zone and the Bar-Lev Line until 1970.

1971
Some 150 M60A1s are purchased by Israel. Israel makes subsequent purchases of M60s prior to the outbreak of war.
Sagger ATGWs are purchased by Egypt and other Arab forces.
May Egyptian armed forces under President Anwar Sadat begin preparing for war against Israel.

1973
6 October Egypt launches a massive invasion of the Sinai across the Suez Canal, coordinating its attack with a Syrian offensive on the Golan Heights.

8 October An IDF counter-attack along the Egyptian defensive positions is driven off with heavy losses of armour, with Sagger missiles taking a significant toll.
11 October Egypt transfers its reserves of armour to the east bank of the Suez, in preparation for an offensive deeper into Sinai.
14 October A new Egyptian offensive aimed at capturing key Sinai passes is destroyed by the resurgent IDF armoured forces.
15–16 October Forces of Ugda *Arik* begin the initial stages of Operation *Gazelle*, the Israeli counter-offensive and crossing of the Suez Canal into Africa. Particularly heavy fighting develops around the Tirtur–Lexicon crossroads and 'Chinese Farm'.
17 October Chinese Farm is eventually cleared, at great cost to IDF armour. Israeli bridgeheads are established across the Suez Canal.
18–21 October Israeli forces make advances both to the north and south on the western side of the Suez Canal, although Ugda *Arik*'s northern advance stalls in the face of fierce Egyptian resistance.
22–25 October United Nations ceasefires progressively come into effect, bringing the Yom Kippur War to a close.

Israeli armour advances during the battle to cross the Suez Canal, 16 October 1973. (AirSeaLand Photos/Cody Images)

DESIGN AND DEVELOPMENT

This book compares very dissimilar, but tactically connected, weapon systems. The difference between the Sagger and the M60, in blunt physical terms, is extreme – one is a 51-tonne (combat loaded weight) MBT and the other is an anti-tank weapon light enough to be carried by a single individual. Yet the considerations behind the development of both systems have been guided by the same and interrelated developments in the arena of armoured warfare. Ultimately, the Sagger and the M60 were in a brutal dialogue with one another, each trying to destroy or survive the other.

THE AT-3 SAGGER

By the end of World War II in 1945, direct-fire anti-tank weapons (at least those used in land warfare) could be separated into three basic types. First, there was the tank itself – after all, a principal purpose of a tank is to destroy another tank. (Within this category there is also the subcategory of tank destroyers.) The tank offered the advantages of mobile firepower combined with high levels of survivability, due to its armour protection. Yet when it came to logistics, transportation and cost, the tank was, and remains, physically and financially draining on its operators. A far cheaper option was the second category of anti-tank weapon: the anti-tank gun, examples of which include the German 7.5cm PaK 40 and 8.8cm FlaK 36 (when used in an anti-tank mode) and the Soviet 57mm ZiS-2 (we might also include recoilless guns in this

category). The anti-tank gun offered the same performance as the mounted tank gun, just without the costs of mechanization, hulls, turrets and armour, and hence could be produced in greater numbers. The trade-off, however, was the greater vulnerability of the gun crew – usually nothing more than a frontal shield provided protection from small-arms fire – and the awkwardness of moving the anti-tank gun quickly from position to position, which generally required an external vehicle.

Then there was the third and final category: the shoulder-launched anti-tank weapon. (I have ignored the anti-tank rifle here, as by World War II tank armour had generally improved to such an extent that these weapons were no longer effective, unless directed at the very weakest spots.) Here World War II produced a variety of highly effective weapons, firing shaped-charge warheads capable of penetrating quite heavy armour. The most famous examples are the American M1 Bazooka, the German *Panzerfaust* and *Panzerschreck*, and the British Projector, Infantry, Anti-Tank (PIAT). Essentially these weapons were meant to be equalizers in the struggle between infantry and tank, giving the infantry a low-cost means to destroy the most formidable armoured adversary. These weapons certainly changed the face of armoured warfare. With the advent of anti-tank rocket-launchers, no longer could tanks operate without close infantry support, particularly in urban areas or around complex defences. If they did so, sooner or later a rocket-armed infantryman would attack from a blind spot and either disable the vehicle or even cause its catastrophic destruction. (During the urban battles in Germany in 1944–45, about 70 per cent of Allied tank losses were caused by *Panzerfaust* or *Panzerschreck* weapons.)

Shoulder-launched anti-tank weapons still had their limitations, however. They were direct-fire weapons firing relatively slow-moving projectiles; trying to hit a fast-moving tank at anything more than point-blank range could be a real challenge. Furthermore, range limitations were severe. A *Panzerfaust*, for example, was essentially a small recoilless gun with a range of little more than 30m – getting into firing range, especially in non-urban settings, was a perilous business, exposing the user to enemy infantry fire plus the full array of weapon systems aboard the tank. The rocket-powered M1 Bazooka, by contrast, had its sights graduated out to 400yd (366m), but in reality operators usually had to get within 100m to catch a tank at the moment it presented its thinner belly, flank or rear armour. So, what shoulder-launched anti-tank weapons provided in terms of proliferation and convenience, they traded against a short, and therefore dangerous, stand-off distance.

What was needed to improve the infantry anti-tank missile was a dramatic improvement in range, but also an equal improvement in the means to deliver the missile with accuracy over range. Here the ever-innovative German engineers hinted at the future. Designed and developed by Ruhrstahl AG in 1943, the X-7 *Rotkäppchen* (Red Riding Hood) was history's first ATGW. The X-7 was the brainchild of Dipl.-Ing. Max Otto Kramer, one of the leading lights in the field of guided weaponry, having designed the Ruhrstahl X-1 (Fritz-X) anti-ship glide bomb (the world's first precision-guided munition) and the Kramer X-4 wire-guided air-to-air missile. The subsequent X-7 was in essence a land-warfare version of the X-4. It was powered by a WASAG 109-506 solid-fuel rocket engine, and had a 2.5kg shaped-charge warhead that was capable of penetrating 205mm of homogenous armour plate. Yet what made the X-7 so truly innovative was its guidance system. The two wings of the X-7 were each connected via wires to a wire-link control system. Once the missile was fired from its special sled launch platform, one member of the three-man X-7 crew used a joystick on the control unit to fly the missile onto the target. Here Kramer had introduced the Manual Command Line of Sight (MCLOS) guidance mechanism that would go on to inform many of the later generations of ATGWs.

The combination of solid-fuel rocket motor and MCLOS guidance system meant that the X-7 could engage targets out to 1.2km, not far off the range of tank guns themselves. Unlike an inert anti-tank gun, however, the X-7's rocket propulsion meant that the missile's trajectory did not fall off over its effective range. The main problem with the X-7, which barely reached beyond the prototype stage and underwent only limited combat testing on the Eastern Front, resided in the operator and the naked eye (there was no sight on the X-7). As military historian Syed Ramsey has noted: 'Accuracy at longer ranges was hampered by the human inability to use stereoscopic vision to judge relative distances after only a few hundred metres. *Rotkäppchen* operators simply could not tell if the missile was heading for the target or had already flown past it' (Ramsey 2016).

The war ended without MCLOS anti-tank weapons progressing beyond mere technological investigation; but the capabilities and potential of these weapon systems, as with so many others developed by the Germans, were not lost on peacetime nations. The first to make a move from theory into proper production were the French, who reflected upon the X-7 from 1948. In 1955 Nord Aviation began producing the SS.10, which not only went into service with the French Army but also the US Army (as the MGM-21A) and, significantly for our discussion, the Israel Defense Forces (IDF). The SS.10 utilized a wire-guided MCLOS system, and had a range of up to 1,600m. It was also man-portable and cheap – the total cost of the missile and its control unit was just 2,140 Francs. The SS.11 was a heavier version intended for helicopter and vehicle deployment, extending the range out to 3,000m. The French also produced, from 1957, the ENTAC (ENgin Téléguidé Anti-Char: Remotely Guided Anti-Tank

Missile), another man-portable weapon that had export success until the mid-1970s, serving customers that included Australia, India, Israel, and again the United States. One noteworthy quality of the ENTAC was that no fewer than ten missile units could be controlled from a single control box.

Other ATGWs soon followed. The British and Australians jointly developed the Malkara in the late 1950s, again using wire-guided MCLOS and fitted not with a shaped-charge warhead, but a 27kg high-explosive squash head (HESH) that could take on most tanks. It was a bulky system, however, and thus could only be mounted on vehicle platforms. Not until the Vickers Vigilant of the 1960s did the British develop a man-portable version. The Swiss and West Germans created the Cobra, which became one of the most successful ATGWs within NATO.

It was also in the 1960s that the Soviets entered the ATGW market in earnest. The first of the communist products was the 3M6 *Shmel* ('Bumblebee'), which began its service life in 1960 and had the NATO reporting name AT-1

The Cobra was one of the postwar generation of anti-tank guided missiles, developed by Oerlikon-Contraves of Switzerland and Bölkow GmbH of West Germany. The first version of the missile had a maximum range of 1,600m, later (1968) upgraded to 2,000m with the Cobra 2000 variant. (Photo by Keystone-France/Gamma-Keystone via Getty Images)

'Snapper'. Keeping with the pace of technological development, the Snapper was a wire-guided MCLOS system with a range out to 2.3km, a distance it took 20 seconds to cover. It was a heavy weapon system – the missile alone had a launch weight of 22.5kg to deliver a 5.4kg High-Explosive Anti-Tank (HEAT) warhead. Thus it was only carried on vehicle mounts, specifically an adapted GAZ-69 light truck or via pop-up launch rails aboard a BRDM-1 armoured reconnaissance vehicle.

The Snapper was inaccurate and difficult to use, although it had reasonable export success. It was soon followed, in 1964, by the 3M11 *Fleyta* ('Flute'), or AT-2 'Swatter'. The Swatter was another heavy system, mounted on BRDM-1 and BRDM-2 infantry fighting vehicles (IFVs) but also on a variety of Soviet attack helicopters. To make it better suited to the aerial platform, and to cope with the extended ranges it offered (the second-generation 9M17 *Skorpion* missile increased the range to 3.5km), the Swatter used MCLOS but with radio command guidance. This did make the Swatter more vulnerable, however, to electronic countermeasures.

As well as two heavy ATGWs in its inventory by the end of the 1960s, the Soviet Union also ended the decade with its first man-portable system – the 9M14 *Malyutka* ('Little One'), or AT-3 Sagger. The exact programme of development for the Sagger is uncertain, cloaked as it was in the secrecy of the Cold War mentality. Most sources list the development effort beginning in July 1961, with design bureaus in Tula and Kolomna working on the project. The specifications required for the weapon were as follows: it had to be capable of being vehicle mounted and/or man-portable; it had to

Once in production, the Sagger ATGW was immediately distributed throughout the Eastern Bloc and to communist client states. This Sagger is being operated by a member of the Czech Army; the image gives a good profile of the missile body (note the jet nozzles straddling the motor and warhead sections) and the 9Sh16 periscope sight. (AirSeaLand Photos/Cody Images)

have a maximum range of 3,000m; it had to deliver a penetration of 200mm of armour at a 60-degree angle; and the weight of the missile should not exceed 10kg. Testing of the new missile continued through the remainder of 1961 and 1962, and the missile as developed by the Kolomna Machine Design Bureau was finally accepted for service on 16 September 1963. The Sagger made its public debut in the Victory Day Parade in Moscow on 9 May 1965.

The Sagger was a pure MCLOS weapon, using a simple wire-guidance system for its entire flight, the missile tracked by the operator to the target via a 9Sh16 periscope sight and a 9S415 joystick control. It carried a 2.6kg HEAT warhead and satisfied the specification requirements with a 3km range. The new weapon had flexibility of mount and deployment options. For the infantry, the 9P111 man-portable fibreglass suitcase launcher system was developed, the suitcase containing the missile

An AT-3 Sagger mounted atop a captured Arab BMP-1 amphibious tracked infantry fighting vehicle, alongside the 73mm 2A28 Grom gun. Although the Sagger technically made the BMP-1 into a tank killer, it was unwise for the vehicles to go toe-to-toe with tanks, without their own armoured support. (AirSeaLand Photos/Cody Images)

components, while the lid could be configured as the missile rail launcher (the control unit was carried separately). For vehicles, 9S428 single-shot launcher units could be attached to BMD/BMD-1 and BMP/BMP-1 IFVs, while a 9P110 six-shot launcher in a retractable rail launcher was carried in the BRDM 4×4 vehicle. (An armoured metal plate covered the launcher in its retracted position.) The Egyptian Army would use all of these configurations during the Yom Kippur War.

Prior to the Yom Kippur War, the Sagger missile went through two main iterations. The first generation of missile was the basic 9M14 *Malyutka* (AT-3A Sagger A). In 1973, however, an improved missile was introduced, the 9M14M *Malyutka-M* (AT-3B Sagger B). This new missile, which became the most prolific model throughout the 1970s and 1980s, weighed a little more than its predecessor on account of an improved rocket motor, which delivered a faster speed (115m/sec) and therefore a quicker flight time to target.

Before we move on to looking at the M60 tank, one interesting historical point about the Sagger was that the Yom Kippur War was not its first combat outing. On 23 April 1973, the North Vietnamese Army deployed small numbers of Soviet-

9K11 *MALYUTKA* (AT-3 SAGGER)

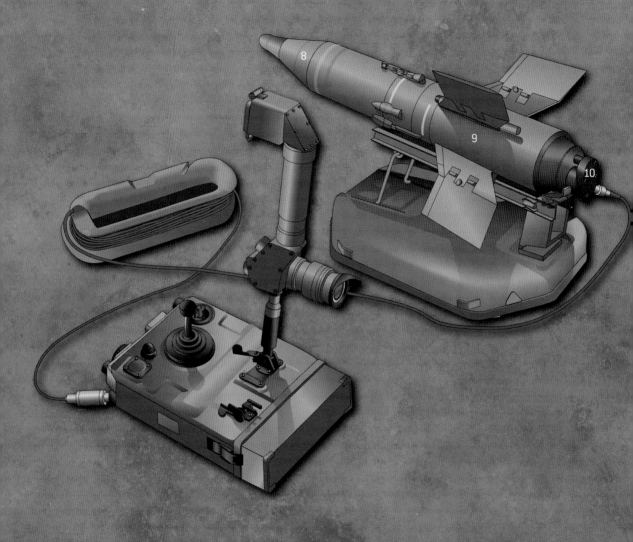

Here we see two views of the 9K11 *Malyutka* (AT-3 Sagger) man-portable system in its classic infantry configuration, as witnessed in Arab hands during the Yom Kippur War. The 9M14 *Malyutka* (AT-3A Sagger A) or improved 9M14M *Malyutka-M* (AT-3B Sagger B) missile came packed within the 9P111 fibreglass suitcase in three main parts: warhead, rocket motor section, and control wire plus connector. To assemble, the suitcase was opened and its contents removed. The lid of the suitcase could then be detached from the body and placed firmly on the ground; the missile launch cradle was then extended on top of the lid surface. The warhead and rocket motor section were connected and latched together, and the assembled missile was then placed onto the launch cradle, the nose of the missile angled upwards. The red control-unit connector on the wire spool was inserted into the port on the very rear of the missile, and the connected cable was unwound from the spool to the required length (up to 15m from the operator). The other end of the cable terminated in a jack, which was plugged into the 9S415 joystick control unit via one of four ports – the operator could fit a total of four missiles to the control unit – which was also fitted with a 9Sh16 periscope sight. The control unit featured a separate battery pack, and when this was connected it powered up the system ready for launch.

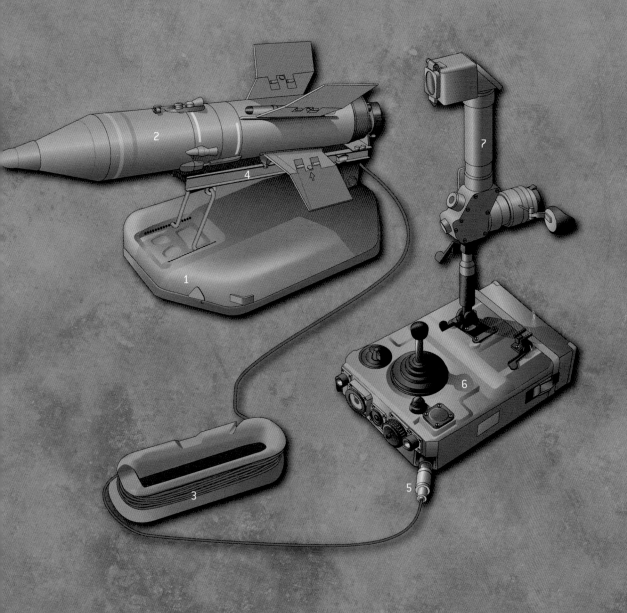

1. 9P111 suitcase missile carrier/launcher (lid with launcher rail)

2. 9M14M *Malyutka-M* missile

3. Missile-to-control unit connecting wire

4. Wire frame launch cradle

5. Control unit connection port (with plug in place)

6. 9S415 joystick control unit

7. 9Sh16 periscope sight

8. Missile warhead section

9. Missile motor section

10. Missile-to-control unit connection port

supplied Saggers against the 20th Tank Regiment of the Army of the Republic of Vietnam. One M48A3 tank – a predecessor of the M60 – and an M113 armoured personnel carrier (APC) were destroyed. Yet the limited numbers of Saggers available, and the different nature of the Vietnamese terrain, meant that the international community was not too alarmed by the presence of this new weapon system; a situation that would change in October 1973.

THE M60

The M60 Patton MBT was the product of an incremental evolution, rather than a sudden leap forward in innovative design. By the time it entered service with the IDF in 1971, the M60 and its upgraded version, the M60A1, represented some of the best developments in gunnery, engine technology and survivability, at least in terms of a mass-production vehicle.

The evolution of the M60 began during World War II, with the M26 Pershing. The M26 was the heaviest tank in the US arsenal by the end of World War II, but in the immediate aftermath of the war – and with the United States now focused on the Soviet armoured threat – it was in need of an upgrade. This it received in the form of improvements to its powerplant, engine, transmission, tracks and various other components to create the M46 Patton. Tank design was evolving quickly, however, spurred not only by the international arms race, but also by the formation of NATO in 1949, with all the requirements for standardization and improvements that involved. During the 1950s, therefore, the M46 Patton received yet another substantial reconfiguration, courtesy of the Chrysler Corporation. The list of modifications, which produced the M48 Patton, was significant. The crew was reduced from five to four (commander, gunner, loader, driver; the M26 had a hull machine gunner); the hull and turret shape and armour were improved to enhance survivability; a new torsion bar suspension was introduced; and an improved 90mm M41 cannon was fitted, with better sighting systems and rangefinding for firing HEAT ammunition.

The M48 was actually something of a stop-gap measure, as the US armed services sought to develop their next generation of MBT. It also had a list of problems, not least that its petrol engine resulted in the tank having an inadequate operating range plus, more alarmingly, a propensity to catch fire easily when struck by enemy fire. Thus the M48 required significant upgrades, and it was these that would lead inexorably to the M60 Patton. The M48A1 added a hand-cranked M1 commander's cupola atop the turret, fitted with a .50-calibre (12.7mm) machine gun and giving the commander better personal protection. The M48A2, meanwhile, received enhanced fire-control systems while, crucially, the M48A3 was fitted with a Continental Motors AVDS-1790 diesel engine, which delivered better power and resistance to catching fire.

Yet still these improvements were deemed insufficient as further data flowed in regarding the capabilities and technologies of potential Soviet tank adversaries, demonstrated in various Cold War conflicts around the globe (the M48 was exported widely to various flashpoints in the Middle East, Africa and East Asia). In the late 1950s it was decided that the key focus of the next wave of improvements had to be

on gunnery, spurred by the examination of a captured Soviet T-54A MBT's 100mm D-10T main gun in Budapest during the Hungarian Revolution of October–November 1956. Although the US Army was looking into the development of a cutting-edge tank called the T95, the cost and long timeline of that programme meant that an interim measure had to be found. This short-term focus became the XM60 programme, launched in June 1958.

The AVDS-1790-2A diesel engine provided the motive force of the M60, but it was really a change in main armament that transformed the M48 into the M60. Trials were conducted to find a new cannon capable of destroying the latest Soviet MBTs, and matching them in terms of range and accuracy. The stand-out weapon from these trials was the British Royal Ordnance 105mm L7 cannon, trumping the 90mm, 100mm and 120mm alternatives. However, adoption of the L7 (as the M68) for the new M60 tank meant that the M48's turret and hull had to be modified to take the weapon. The turret was increased in size, becoming longer and flatter to retain as low a silhouette as possible. The fire-control system was upgraded to include the advanced M131D ballistic computer, which calculated and automatically applied elevation via the M10 ballistic drive, the information coming from the tank commander's range calculations using the M17 stereoscopic rangefinder and the gunner's selection of

US Army M60 Patton MBTs in convoy during the first annual NATO Exercise *Reforger* (REturn of FORces to GERmany) in West Germany in January 1969. Note the large Xenon searchlight over the barrel; this feature was omitted on most Israeli Magach 6s. (Photo by Rolls Press/Popperfoto/Getty Images)

ammunition type. Other modifications to achieve the M60 standard included an improved Cadillac Gage hydraulic system to cope with the increased recoil of the 105mm main gun, and larger hull fuel tanks to provide a greater range (up to 193km, depending on the terrain), but by far the most visible distinction was the introduction of the M19 commander's weapon station (CWS) cupola. This feature meant that the commander could retain better awareness and protection with the hatch 'buttoned-down', and it also featured a .50-calibre M85 machine gun. There were some modifications to the hull shape. The front of the hull was changed from a round shape to a sharp wedge, with a greater angle of frontal deflection against enemy shells. The frontal armour initially selected was to be a siliceous core type, but the cost consequences of both the armour itself and the required modifications to hull and turret shape meant that this armour was dropped in favour of cast steel. The transmission was enhanced and the suspension improved through the addition of shock absorbers to number 1 and number 6 wheels, which improved the crew's experience of cross-country undulations.

The M60 entered production in 1959, and service in the US forces the following year. Yet the rush to get tracks onto earth meant that there remained issues to resolve in the new tank, hence it almost straight away entered an upgrade programme. Modifications implemented between 1960 and 1963 resulted in the M60A1, which was the dominant variant of the M60 in production from 1962 until the early 1980s.

One of the major features that distinguished the M60A1 from the M60 was that the former had an even larger turret, with a more elongated frontal section. The change in the frontal shape provided additional deflection protection against enemy fire, while the greater overall interior space meant an increase in main-gun ammunition stowage from 60 rounds (M60) to 63 rounds. The M60A1 also had an improved 750hp AVDS-1790-2C diesel engine with Allison CD-850-6/6A powershift crossdrive transmission. There were a host of other minor changes for the M60A1 version and subsequent upgrades, including upgraded gunner's optics, particularly the M32/M35 sights that provided both the gunner and the commander with night-vision capabilities. A T-shaped bar control for the driver (as opposed to the steering wheel on the standard M60) gave improved levels of steering control, and shock absorbers were fitted to the number 2 wheels to cope with the increased weight of the new turret. A Top Loading Air Cleaner (TLAC) add-on extracted dust and dirt from the engine to improve its lifespan. Another significant add-on came in late 1972 with the introduction of the Add-On Stabilization (AOS) kit for the main gun, giving gyroscopic stabilization of the gun while the tank was on the move, consequently improving both survivability and first-round hit probability.

THE M60 IN ISRAELI SERVICE

M48 tanks began entering the IDF arsenal during the early 1960s, sold by the United States to Israel between 1960 and 1964 via West Germany to avoid political issues, although once these trade arrangements became known to the media this trade route was shut down and the United States opted to supply Israel directly. Regardless of their path of delivery, however, the M48 gave good service to the Israelis on the Sinai and Jordanian fronts in the Six-Day War of June 1967. The 105mm main-gun upgrade was especially appreciated, as this gave the IDF the capability to outgun Soviet-built

T-34, T-54 and IS-3 tanks and SU-100 tank destroyers. But the evident advances in Soviet tank technology throughout the 1960s and into the 1970s meant that the IDF arsenal had to keep up with the pace of development, hence the M60 was acquired.

The M60A1 entered service with the IDF in 1971 as the Magach 6A, when a batch of 150 of the tanks were purchased for the Israeli Armored Corps (IAC). The M60A1 was at the time one of the most sophisticated tanks on the Western market, and given the heavy Arab investment in modern Soviet armour, it was a judicious purchase by the Israelis. Note that the IDF had also, by 1973, upgraded 709 of its British Centurion tanks (known as Sh'ot Cal in IDF service) with the 105mm L7 main gun and the M48/M60 diesel engine. The other tanks in the IDF arsenal at this time were unmodernized Centurions, M48s (including versions with 105mm main guns), captured T-54/T-55s and upgraded Sherman M50/M51s.

As noted above, deliveries of the M60A1 to Israel began in 1971, adding a further element of modernization to IDF armour. Yet in the immediate run-up to the Yom Kippur War, and indeed while the war itself was unfolding, the IDF took deliveries not only of more M60A1s but also of older M60s, which were accessible from redundant US stocks. In Israeli hands, the US tanks were either virtually unmodified

On 7 May 1973, Jerusalem hosted a spectacular Independence Day parade, to celebrate 25 years of the State of Israel. Part of the military parade was this drive-past by some of the 150 M60A1/Magach 6A tanks provided by the United States in 1971. (Bettmann/Getty Images)

19

from their delivery state (apart from, say, swapping out communications equipment) or had some more substantial local adaptations. One of the key changes was the swapping out of the US-installed M19 CWS on the M60 for the indigenous Urdan commander's cupola. The commander's position in the turret was a hot topic for the IDF armoured forces. Traditionally, the preference was for Israeli tank commanders to stand up through the turret hatches even in combat, the benefits of the greater all-round awareness and quicker reactions from the commander being deemed worth the additional risk from enemy fire. The experience of the Six-Day War, however, placed a question mark over this policy, on account of the heavy losses among tank commanders. It was a not uncommon, and dreadful, experience for Israeli tank crews to suddenly find a headless commander dropping down into the turret and hull, having been decapitated by a passing shell or cannon rounds. The IDF policy shifted

M60A1/MAGACH 6A, 1st BATTALION, 600th RESERVE ARMORED BRIGADE

The Magach 6A shown here belongs to the 1st Battalion (denoted by the single white band around the main-gun barrel) of the 600th Reserve Armored Brigade, the company indicated by the inverted 'V' on the side of the hull (V indicates the 1st Company). This is one of the tanks that remained largely unmodified from its US-supplied format, with the M19 commander's weapon station (CWS) cupola atop the main turret, armed with a .50-calibre M85 machine gun; note also the multiple vision blocks around the base of the CWS. Spare track links are carried on the outside of the turret. These provided ready links in case of track damage and also gave (at least over a limited portion of the hull) extra protection against enemy fire, providing an additional stand-off distance from the hull to reduce shaped-charge warhead penetration. Note also the bustle rack around the rear of the hull. Not only was this useful for storing additional equipment, but by placing sandbags here it boosted protection over the most weakly armoured part of the turret.

M60A1/MAGACH 6A SPECIFICATIONS

Crew: 4 (commander, driver, gunner, loader)
Length: 9.42m (gun forward)
Height: 3.28m
Width: 3.62m
Engine: 750hp Continental AVDS-1790-2C V12, air-cooled twin-turbo diesel
Combat weight: 51.3 tonnes
Power-to-weight ratio: 14.2hp/tonne
Maximum road speed: 48km/h

Transmission: Allison CD-850-6/6A powershift crossdrive
Range: 500km
Fuel capacity: 1,420 litres
Fuel consumption: 3.1 litres/km
Ground pressure: 0.87kg/cm^2
Armament: 105mm L7 main gun; 7.62mm M240 coaxial machine gun; .50-calibre M85 machine gun in commander's cupola
Main-gun ammunition: 63 rounds

9.42m (gun forward)

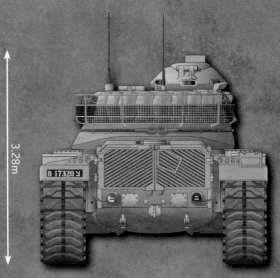

3.28m

3.62m

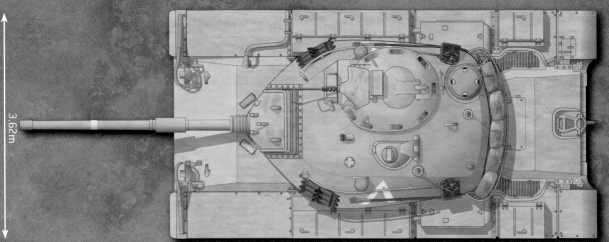

An IDF M60 on manoeuvres in the Sinai Desert during the 1970s. The Royal Ordnance 105mm L7 main gun stands out in this image. This popular gun was fitted to many other tanks, including the updated M48A3, the Centurion, the German Leopard 1 and the first variant of the M1 Abrams. (AirSeaLand Photos/Cody Images)

more towards the survivability end of the equation, hence the appeal of the M60 tank with its CWS. Some felt, however, that the US cupola was still too prominent, raising the profile of the tank and by implication the risk to the commander. The Urdan cupola had a very low profile in its design, and was in fact originally designed to fit the M48 turret. Unlike the M19 CWS, the Urdan cupola did not have an integral machine gun as part of its design. It did, however, have a pintle-mount bracket on its outer rim, which could be used for taking a Browning .30-calibre machine gun or a .50-calibre machine gun.

Some Israeli M60A1s also received field modifications by IAC crews. Most of the tanks had the original M19 CWS in place, although in some instances the M85 machine gun was removed from its mount, in preference for an externally mounted .30-calibre machine gun. In other instances .50-calibre M2HB machine guns were externally fitted to the turret. One of the advantages of using externally mounted machine guns was that they gave the commander more immediate target acquisition, particularly when looking for Sagger teams in the expanse of the Sinai Desert. Under intense fire, however, the commander was better advised to lower himself down into the turret and close the hatch.

The M60A1 was a fine tank but at the beginning of 1973 it had yet to prove itself in war, although it was continuing the proven combat ancestry of the M48 series. What the new tank had never faced was the Sagger ATGM. Indeed, given the scale of the Arab deployment of these weapon systems, this was in essence true for all Israeli armour.

THE STRATEGIC SITUATION

The Yom Kippur War, and indeed much of subsequent Middle Eastern history to date, was framed by the Six-Day War. On 5 June 1967, Israel launched one of the most audacious pre-emptive military land-grabs in history. Taking the initiative in the face of months of increasing tension with the surrounding Arab states, the IDF delivered a lightning, multi-front campaign against Egypt, Syria and Jordan. It was an action characterized by brilliance and aggressive confidence. The dash and tactical skill of the IDF meant that by the time a ceasefire was declared on 11 June, Israeli forces had taken the Sinai (right up to the Suez Canal) from Egypt, the Golan Heights from Syria, and East Jerusalem and the Gaza Strip from Jordan.

The conquests of the Six-Day War provided Israel with the psychological security of a wide buffer zone between the homeland and the Arab states, a strategic depth Israel was keen to retain despite subsequent international pressure. On the other side, Arab military and political pride had taken a severe battering, and with Israel now within potentially easy reach of major Arab urban centres, including Cairo and Damascus, the governments of Gamal Nasser (Egypt) and Hafez al-Assad (Syria) looked for a strategy to reclaim their lost territory. To do so, military pressure had to be maintained on Israel.

What became known as the 'War of Attrition' – a rumbling series of border clashes around the Suez Canal Zone – began small, with pinprick clashes initiated by both sides, but in 1968 Nasser declared the official start of the campaign, and the fighting intensified. Egypt's intended attrition was real – 1,424 Israeli soldiers were killed in action between 15 June 1967 and 8 August 1970, plus another 2,569 wounded – but it worked both ways, with total Arab losses from Israeli responses possibly exceeding 20,000 dead, wounded and captured.

Prompted by the onset of the War of Attrition, Israel recognized the imperative to consolidate and defend the new front line in Sinai. The physical product of this understanding was what became known as the Bar-Lev Line, named after IDF Chief of Staff Haim Bar-Lev. Developed principally by Major-General Avraham 'Bren' Adan, this $300 million programme of defensive works would set the immediate tactical scenario for the fighting in the Sinai in 1973. The principal elements of the Bar-Lev Line consisted of 15 *Maozim* strongpoints that ran the entire 160km distance from the Mediterranean Sea to the Gulf of Suez, with roughly 8–11km between each strongpoint. The *Maozim* were positioned to protect significant points along the Sinai front line, particularly the east–west road junctions as they crossed the north–south Artillery Road, which ran in parallel with the Suez Canal about 10km inland. The *Maozim* were not heavily manned – each typically had a platoon-strength unit of about 40–50 men, dropping down to about 20 men during quiet periods – but they were well sited, well-protected by frontal earthworks, trenches, barbed wire and bunkers, and well-armed with heavy machine guns and mortars. They also had prepared firing ramps for armour; when required, the tanks would mount the ramps, giving them an elevated firing position down onto the Suez Canal. Mirroring the *Maozim* strongpoints roughly 8km inland were some 15 larger *Taozim* strongholds, built into a line of rough desert hills. Each of these positions was capable of holding a company of troops, plus small numbers of tanks were kept in readiness. Larger amounts of reserve armour were held along the Artillery Road and the parallel Lateral Road further back in the desert.

The year 1970 brought two game-changers. First, in August the United States managed to broker a ceasefire between the two sides. The second, which occurred the next month, was that Gamal Nasser died and into his place stepped Anwar Sadat. The new President of Egypt was something of a challenge and enigma for the Israelis. More diplomatic, quieter, apparently even sensitive, when compared to Nasser, Sadat honoured the 1970 ceasefire (at first) and opened up negotiations with President Nixon of the United States, seeking to use international pressure to reclaim Egyptian territory lost during the Six-Day War. In this climate of detente (Nixon was also in more prolific communication with his Soviet counterpart, Leonid Brezhnev), Sadat started pulling away from the Soviet Union, in the spring of 1972 even asking the many Soviet 'advisors' to leave; most did so, although a key motivation was also to encourage the Soviets to provide Egypt with more advanced weaponry.

Many in the Israeli government and the Israeli AMAM, the Military Intelligence Directorate headed by Major-General Eli Zeira, felt they had the measure of Sadat as someone who was weak and who could be contained. Sadat quickly became disillusioned with the lack of progress in terms of peace initiatives, so his talk and momentum increasingly returned to a focus on making war again. In October 1972, he re-opened his interactions with the Soviets via Minister of War General Ahmad Ismail Ali, who secured the resupply of weapon systems. He also announced to his army High Command that Egyptian forces should mobilize for war, which would come soon.

The chief architect of Operation *Badr* – the Egyptian plan to cross the Suez Canal and seize the Bar-Lev Line – was Lieutenant-General Saad El Shazly, who became Chief of Staff of the Egyptian Armed Forces on 16 May 1971. Overcoming resistance

from other commanders, El Shazly, with Sadat's backing, proposed a limited two-front campaign (Egyptian and Syrian fronts) with manageable objectives, exercising restraint against the grandstanding ambition that had brought Arab defeat so often in the past.

In its broadest brushstrokes, the plan broke down as follows. First, a programme of deception would mask the build-up to Operation *Badr* from the Israelis. For example, from 1971 Sadat made warlike proclamations so frequently that they ceased to be taken seriously by the IDF, who came to treat such rhetoric as mere posturing. Second, simultaneous attacks would be launched on the Sinai and Syrian fronts, overstretching the Israeli capacity to respond. On the Sinai front, the Egyptian Second and Third armies would make a combat crossing of the Suez Canal, take the Bar-Lev Line defences, and break out beyond and form shallow but broad defensible bridgeheads against which any Israeli counter-attack would shatter. Third, from their defensive positions, the Egyptian forces could fight exactly the sort of attrition-heavy, prolonged conflict the Israelis wished to avoid, forcing an international diplomatic settlement. Sadat himself said of *Badr*: 'I want us to plan [the offensive] within our capabilities, nothing more. Cross the canal and hold even ten centimetres of the Sinai. I'm exaggerating, of course, but that will help me greatly and alter completely the political situation internationally and within Arab ranks' (quoted in El Shazly 2003: 106).

On Saturday 6 October 1973, the opening day of Operation *Badr* in the Sinai, the IDF and Egypt brought very different capabilities to the table. Looking at the actual battle zone, Israel had about 8,000 infantry present (*c*.600 of them on the Bar-Lev Line), plus about 350 tanks in the 252nd Armored Division, or Ugda *Albert*, after its commander Major-General Avraham Albert Mandler. In reserve were the 162nd Reserve Armored Division (Ugda *Bren*; Major-General Avraham 'Bren' Adan),

An Egyptian T-55 tank rolls through the desert on manoeuvres. The T-55 and the more modern T-62 were the principal armoured threats faced by the IDF during the Yom Kippur War. Both were effective MBTs, illustrated by the fact that the IDF put captured examples into service with the IAC. (AirSeaLand Photos/Cody Images)

143rd Reserve Armored Division (Ugda *Arik*; Major-General Ariel 'Arik' Sharon) and the 146th Reserve Armored Division (Ugda *Kalman*; Brigadier-General Kalman Magen). Together all these forces constituted the IDF Southern Command. Within the 143rd Reserve Armored Division were the IAC M60A1/Magach 6A tanks, contained within the 600th Reserve Armored Brigade (111 tanks) under Colonel Tuvia Raviv and the 87th Armored Reconnaissance Battalion (24 tanks) led by Lieutenant-Colonel Ben-Zion 'Bentzi' Carmeli. The 401st Armored Brigade also relied heavily on M60s.

On the other side of the Suez Canal, the Egyptians had amassed an extremely potent force. The Second Field Army (Major-General Mohammed Sa'ad Ma'amon; Northern Canal Zone) and Third Field Army (Major-General Mohammed Abd El Al Mona'am Wasel) together contained 90,000 infantry, although only 32,000 would actually be committed on the first day of attack, and more than 500 tanks.

The numbers were stacked in the Arabs' favour, but the experience of the Six-Day War had taught Sadat and his military leaders that numerical superiority did not equate to victory. The Egyptians recognized that they could not go toe-to-toe with either the Israeli Air Force (IAF) or the IAC and come out the winner. What was needed was a different approach to equalize the odds. For the air campaign, Nasser then Sadat had pressured the Soviets to supply a sophisticated umbrella of S-75 Dvina (SA-2 'Guideline') and S-125 Neva/Pechora (SA-3 'Goa') SAM systems and MiG-21 'Fishbed' fighter squadrons, plus some 2,500 AA gun systems. Using the same logic at ground level, the Egyptians bolstered each of their infantry divisions with at least 48 Sagger missiles, plus 314 RPG-7s to cover the 0–500m 'dead ground' that the Sagger could not handle. All of the anti-tank missiles within each division were collected into an ATGW battalion, giving the infantry division a powerful tank-killing tool.

The Yom Kippur War brought together two different approaches to armoured warfare. One, the Israeli, focused on the supremacy of the tank itself as a vehicle for deciding the battle. The other, Arab approach (Saggers were also heavily deployed by the Syrians on the Golan Heights) sought to reduce the tank's authority by subduing it in a wide zone of lethality, created by the ATGWs and the RPG-7s. It was an unprecedented clash.

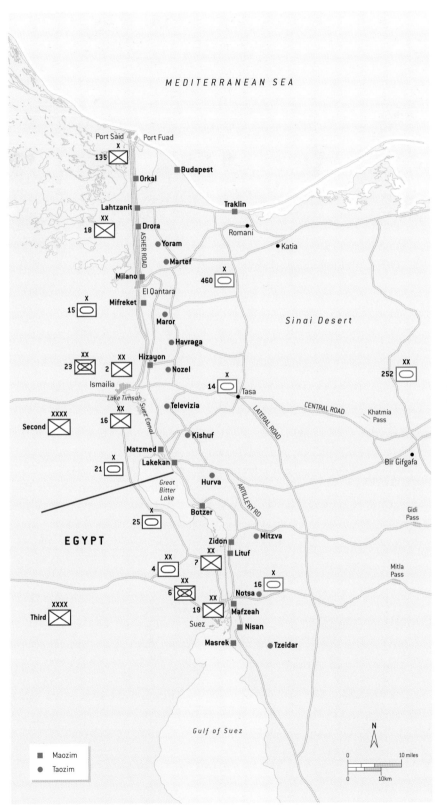

This map of the dispositions of the Egyptian and Israeli forces on the eve of battle on 6 October 1973 strikingly conveys the scale of the threat gathered against the IDF. Two Egyptian field armies – true combined-arms forces of infantry, armour and artillery – were amassed on the western side of the Suez Canal, ready to attack across it and establish a shallow but well-defended strip of territory on the eastern side. The Israelis' main line of defence in the Sinai comprised the 15 *Maozim* strongpoints and 15 *Taozim* strongholds that together constituted the Bar-Lev Line, but these were not heavily manned and the spaces between the positions provided avenues for the Egyptians to bypass and surround the strongholds. IDF armour of the 252nd Armored Division was available in the Sinai, but largely held back in reserve positions further east; it would take time for them to respond fully to an emerging crisis in the Suez Canal Zone.

TECHNICAL SPECIFICATIONS

AT-3 SAGGER

One of the chief virtues of the Sagger system was, and indeed remains, its portability and therefore its battlefield convenience. The missile itself weighs just 10.9kg (slightly more than the original specifications required by the Soviet Defence Ministry), although the 9P111 launcher suitcase plus the fully assembled control unit add another 30.9kg. In strictest military terms, therefore, the Sagger system in its entirety is not classed as 'man-portable', but a two- or three-man team could transport the weapon perfectly well. The length of the assembled missile is 860mm and it has a wingspan of 393mm.

The Sagger is an MCLOS – Manual Command Line of Sight – weapon, which means that the operator must fly the missile visually onto the target. Visual acquisition of the missile in flight is provided by a red-burning flare located on the fibreglass casing of the missile, situated between two of the stabilizing fins. At ranges of 500–1,000m, the best policy for the operator is simply to use open sight to guide the missile to its target, and not the 9Sh16 periscope sight. Up to 1,000m, the human eye retains its spatial awareness enough to make accurate adjustments. At ranges

The Sagger system shown here (minus the 9P111 suitcase launcher) was one of many captured by Israeli forces during the later stages of the Yom Kippur War. The outer casing of the missile itself was made of fibreglass, to keep the weight manageable. (AirSeaLand Photos/Cody Images)

9M14M (AT-3B SAGGER B) MISSILE

The heart of the armour-defeating 9M14M missile is a 9N110M1 HEAT warhead, capped by a 9E236 impact fuze. A cone of copper sits behind the warhead nose, the open end of the cone pointing forward and with explosive blocks stacked around its outer body. When the missile makes contact with the enemy vehicle or position, the fuze detonates the explosives; this in turn blasts the copper cone inwards into its own cavity, in the process liquefying the metal and forming a hypersonic jet of metal particles travelling forward along its own axis. The 'slug' of molten metal forms a highly effective armour penetrator, punching through via a combination of speed and extreme temperature (c.430°C). In the case of the 9M14M missile, its maximum armour penetration is 400mm, although actual penetration depends on the type and angle of armour, the angle at which the missile strikes, and whether or not the missile detonates prior to contact with the armour itself, such as if it strikes a wire cage or external attachments.

The motive power to take the Sagger from launch to target is provided by the 9M14 motor. This consists of two units: a booster motor, which rapidly takes the missile up to its 115m/sec flight velocity, and a sustainer motor, which maintains the speed of flight to the target. Note that the rocket motor vents through four obliquely angled nozzles around the circumference of the booster motor. The angle of each nozzle, plus that of the missile fins themselves, imparts a clockwise spin stabilization at 8.5 revolutions per second. This spin, combined with the instant ignition of the fuel stick by an ignition charge, ensures that the missile doesn't plough into the ground a short distance from the launcher. The sustainer motor takes over within 500m, and vents through two steerable nozzles. It is these nozzles that receive the steering instructions from the operator at the control unit. The range of the 9M14M missile is 3km, this range dictated by the 3,000m of command wire spooled up inside the body of the missile. When the missile is fired, the control end of the wire is linked to the joystick control unit via the connector plug, which remains behind on the launcher unit after launch.

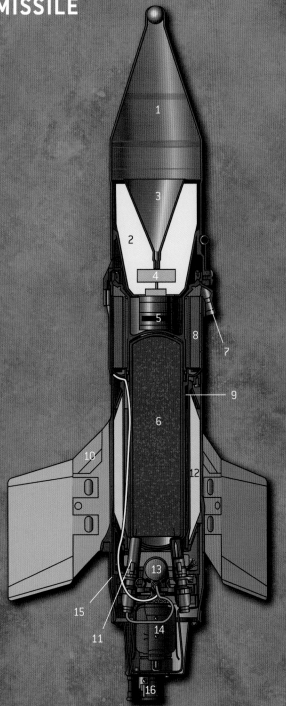

1. Hardened steel head
2. Explosive content
3. Metal-lined conical hollow
4. Booster charge
5. 9E236 nose-sensing base fuze
6. Fuel stick
7. Venturi nozzle
8. Boost motor
9. Sustainer motor
10. Folding stabilizer fins
11. High-pressure gas bleed system (to power steering gear)
12. Wire spool housing
13. Steering gear
14. Gyroscope housing
15. Fibreglass case
16. Connection plug

beyond 1,000m, however, the operator would turn to optical tools, in this case the 9Sh16 periscope sight, keeping the crosshairs on the target while at the same time making adjustments to the front joystick of the control unit to direct the missile onto the crosshairs, and thereby strike the target. Note that this is an action requiring some skill. Subsequent evolutions of ATGWs merely required the operator to keep the crosshairs on the target, and the missile automatically tracked to that aiming point. With the early Saggers, however, the operator had both to maintain crosshairs alignment and fly the missile accurately to those crosshairs, a feat that required considerable practice to do well. The Sagger also has a very 'jumping' style of directional flight, the missile bobbing and weaving its way to the target, altering direction with each command adjustment plus itself automatically adjusting for effects such as missile spin.

One further complication for the Sagger operator is that the missile has a minimum as well as a maximum range. On launch, the missile climbs steeply under the powerful impulse of the booster motor, then drops again as the sustained-flight motor takes over. This means that for the first 500m the missile climbs up beyond the operator's periscope line of sight, and then only drops back into it at about 500m. Thus the first 500m is essentially 'dead ground' for the Sagger, and this was a key reason why both Soviet doctrine and Arab tactical policy allowed for numerous RPG-7 operators to work alongside the Sagger teams, to plug the gap in the Sagger's range.

Another key consideration for the Sagger user is the flight time to target, especially at maximum range. The flight time out to 3,000m would be up to 30 seconds, which in combat conditions – i.e. under fire – was a long time in which to maintain concentration and make the fine adjustments necessary to guide the missile onto the target. In the Yom Kippur War, it was this period of guidance to the target that became the window of opportunity for the Israelis to implement countermeasures to the Sagger.

M60A1

For the Israelis, one of the chief advantages of the M60A1 (our main focus here, as the most prolific of the IDF M60 variants), and of purchasing US and European tanks in general, was the fact that such vehicles had been through intensive testing and evaluation phases before they were shipped to the customer. For example, from 25 April to 4 August 1972, a US-production M60A1 was pulled out for extensive testing at Aberdeen Proving Ground in Maryland, the tank being specifically tested for endurance, construction, automotive soundness, turret functionality and gunnery. A number of issues were identified, the most significant of which were:

> First, the shifting control hasp is readily dislodged from the quadrant and the shifting and steering controls can then be inadvertently moved with possible injury to personnel, if the engine is running. Second, both tracks guide against the inner edges of the outer sprockets causing excessive wear on the sprockets and the outer edges of the track shoes. (Kotras 1972: i)

Interestingly, it was noted that these shortcomings 'have been observed on prior produced M60A1 tanks' (Kotras 1972: i), which means that these problems were passed on to the Israelis in the first batch of M60A1s delivered in 1971. Nevertheless, although the M60A1 did not emerge from the Yom Kippur War with a spotless reputation for survivability and mechanical reliability, with the support of Israeli engineering personnel it did give dependable performance.

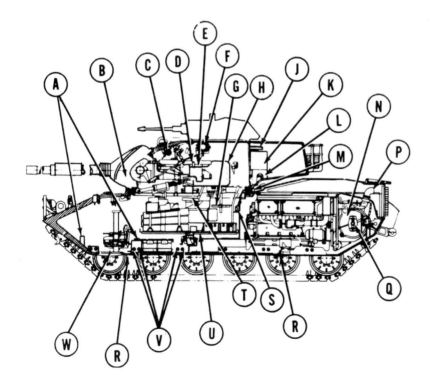

A US Army manual diagram points out key interior components of the M60A1 tank: (A) headlight stowage brackets; (B) 105mm main-gun mount; (C) replenisher assembly; (D) breech operating handle; (E) loader's guard; (F) rangefinder; (G) commander's platform; (H) gunner's guard; (J) observation seat (stowed); (K) radio equipment; (L) oddment tray; (M) inflatable hull-to-turret seal; (N) transmission; (P) engine exhaust elbows; (Q) universal joint; (R) hull drain valves; (S) engine air cleaner intakes; (T) gunner's seat; (U) turret platform; (V) torsion bars (total of 12); (W) driver's escape hatch. (US Army)

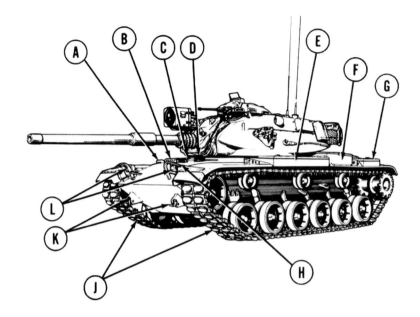

External features of the M60A1: (A) personnel heater exhaust outlet; (B) driver's vision blocks; (C) driver's hatch; (D) driver's periscope cover; (E) fender stowage box; (F) engine air cleaner; (G) rear fender stowage box; (H) fire extinguisher release handles; (J) track; (K) towhooks; (L) headlights. (US Army)

The physical fundamentals of the M60A1 were a gun-forward length of 9.42m, a height of 3.28m and a width of 3.62m, with a ground clearance of 0.46m. Maximum combat weight was 51.3 tonnes, with a ground pressure of 0.87kg/cm^2. Armament consisted of the 105mm L7 main gun, a 7.62mm M240 coaxial machine gun, and a .50-calibre M85 machine gun in the commander's cupola.

Looking more generally at life inside the M60A1, it had a crew of four. The commander sat in the rear right of the turret, beneath the commander's cupola. The gunner and loader both occupied the main fighting compartment of the hull, with the gunner on the right and the loader on the left. Beneath them, down at the front of the hull, was the driver. The driver was responsible for handling the vehicle's Continental AVDS-1790-2C V12 air-cooled twin-turbo diesel engine, which produced 750hp and pushed the tank to a maximum speed of 48km/h. Steering was via a T-bar arrangement, and the transmission offered two forward and one reverse gears. Vision for the driver was achieved via either a frontal hatch or, when the hatch was closed, an M27 periscope.

Furthest away from the driver was the commander, surrounded by an impressive battery of controls principally related to the commander's gunnery and communications functions. His M17A1 rangefinder allowed him to take control of aiming both the 105mm main gun and the M240 coaxial machine gun, while additional controls gave him the facility to override the gunner and fire the weapons himself. He could also operate and fire the M85 machine gun mounted in the overhead cupola. Standard communications equipment on the tanks as delivered from the United States were a 920-channel Receiver-Transmitter RT-246/VRC, a Receiver R-422/VRC (this allowed the commander to monitor one channel while keeping the Receiver-Transmitter tuned to another), plus an audio frequency amplifier to boost the sound quality of the crew intercom, external interphone and the radio.

For the gunner, most of his controls were naturally related to aiming and firing the 105mm main gun. As noted previously, the 105mm main gun on the M60 tank series

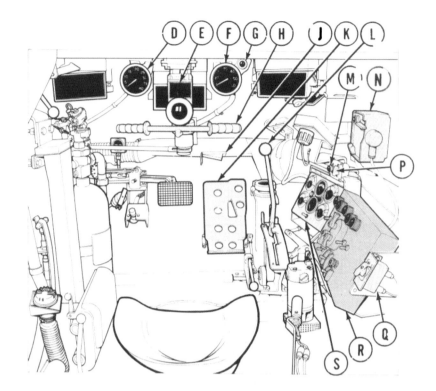

Driver controls in the M60A1: (D) tachometer/hour meter; (E) IR Periscope M24; (F) speedometer/odometer; (G) powerplant warning lamp; (H) steering control; (J) heater air outlet door; (K) accelerator pedal; (L) transmission shift control; (M) smoke generator indicator light; (N) intercom control panel; (P) smoke generator switch; (Q) air cleaner blower switch; (R) master control panel; (S) Indicator panel. (US Army)

was the L7 cannon developed by the British Royal Ordnance Factories as a replacement for the 84mm 20-pounder main gun originally fitted to the Centurion tank. (The IDF also went into battle with 105mm Centurions.) The L7 has a rifled bore 52 calibres in length (5.89m) and weighs 1.28 tonnes. In the hands of an experienced crew, the L7 could be fired at a rate of 10rd/min; as we shall see, this rate of fire became crucial as a counter-response by the tank crews to the Sagger threat.

For the gunner using this weapon, the primary battlefield observation device was the 8× M105D telescope sight. Within this the gunner could select a reticle type suited to one of three ammunition types: Armour-Piercing Discarding Sabot (APDS), High-Explosive Plastic (HEP – another name for the HESH warhead) or HEAT. The gunner also had access to a range of technologies to make his job of target acquisition, aiming and firing more reliable and quicker. A US Department of Defense (DOD) document from 1980 explains the role of the Add-On Stabilization kit, noted earlier, and the support provided by the rangefinder and the M13A2 ballistic computer:

When vehicles are equipped with add-on stabilization, the 105mm gun and coaxial 7.62mm machine gun may be used in any one of three modes of control: (1) power-with-stabilization-on, (2) power-with-stabilization-off, and (3) manual. In the power-with-stabilization-on mode, the gunner's aim on target is automatically retained while the vehicle is in motion. This mode provides a fire-on-the-move capability. The power-with-stabilization-off option eliminates needless exercise of the stabilization system and provides a back up power mode. The manual back up system permits the crew to aim and fire the weapons should the electrical/hydraulical subsystems malfunction. The rangefinder is a full-field coincidence image instrument used as the ranging device of the primary direct sighting and fire control system. Range information from the rangefinder is fed into the ballistic computer through a shaft. The ballistic computer is a mechanically driven unit that permits ammunition selection, range correction, and superelevation correction. The ballistic computer receives range input and, through the use of cams and gears, provides superelevation information to the superelevation actuator. The superelevation actuator adds sufficient hydraulic fluid to the elevating mechanism to correctly position the gun. (US Army 1980: 1-1)

The Add-On Stabilization kit, rangefinder and the ballistic computer together made for a sophisticated gunnery system that allowed the gunner or commander to engage targets from about 500m through to 4,000m, although 2,000m was the optimal range for penetration of heavy armour when using APDS rounds. Indeed, the effective range of the 105mm main gun was affected by everything from the type of ammunition fired through to the air temperature on the battlefield. The ballistic computer went a long way in helping the gunner to calculate all the variables for the precision placement of a shot.

Supporting the gunner in his endeavours was the loader, whose job it was to load the right ammunition type based on instructions from the gunner. The loader would take the ammunition from one of the ready racks around the tank interior. Compared to the commander, driver and gunner, the loader had relatively few controls to consider. This is not to suggest any relative unimportance – the speed at which the loader could locate the shells, extract them from their ready racks, and ram them home into the breech could make the literal difference between life and death for all members of the crew. To the left side of the gun breech was a handle for opening the breech; a plunger button on the top of the breech released the breech lock. Next to the breech operating handle was a main-gun safety switch, which allowed the main gun to fire electrically when in the forward position, plus a trip lever that moved the safety switch from 'fire' to 'safe' whenever the main gun was fired. Above the loader's head, on the turret ceiling, were controls for his communications (intercom and radio transmission), heating controls, plus the traverse lock handle, which locked or unlocked the turret for traverse.

The M60A1 was designed for the multi-threat environments of conventional Cold War battlefields. Its technical capabilities and the skills of its crew therefore had to merge into one efficiently functioning entity. In the *Operator's Manual* for the M60A1 (RISE) the purpose of the M60A1 is simply described as 'A moveable main battle tank designed to attack and defeat enemy armour and other targets.' It then goes on to list the 'Capability and Features':

Operates within a nuclear-biological-chemical environment
Moves rapidly over cross country terrains
Provides close infantry support
Provides indirect fire, same as artillery
Allows fire-on-the-move from stabilized turret
Fords water up to 48 inches (1.2 meters) deep without water fording kit
Fords water up to 8 feet (2.4 meters) deep when kit installed
Provides night sighting during lowlight levels
Provides choice of white searchlight or security infrared searchlight

M60/M60A1 AMMUNITION TYPES

In 1973, the M60/M60A1 tanks fired four main types of 105mm shell. Note that all of these shells were of the unitary cartridge type and were fired by electrical ignition.

The 105mm APDS-T M392 (**A**), a hypervelocity armour-piercing round, was a saboted round, in which a sub-calibre tungsten-carbide penetrator was encased in a sheath (the sabot) that fitted the calibre of the main gun, but which dropped away from the penetrator once both components left the muzzle. This arrangement allowed a lighter, more aerodynamic projectile to be fired than a full-calibre projectile would permit, and at higher velocities. Note that the penetrator itself had no explosive content; it inflicted its destruction purely through kinetic energy. A tracer component was added to the base of the shell to allow the gunner and commander to observe the shell in flight.

The 105mm HEAT-T M456 (**B**), a HEAT round with tracer, was a shaped-charge warhead type that combined penetration with explosive effects. The stand-off spike at the nose ensured that the shell exploded at the correct distance from the armour surface, to allow the penetrating jet of molten metal to form itself properly.

The 105mm HEP-T M393A1 (**C**) was a HESH-type shell with tracer. On impact, the explosive content of the warhead was plastered over the surface of the armour then exploded by the base-detonating fuze. The blast effect sent shock waves through the armour, either blowing through it or creating 'spall' (lethal fragments of detached metal) to blow off the interior of the armour at high velocities, inflicting casualties and destroying equipment.

The 105mm Smoke M416 (**D**) was loaded with white phosphorus (WP). On impact with the target, the base fuze would trigger a C4 explosive bursting charge that ruptured the shell and dispersed the WP over some distance. In contact with air, WP produces a dense white smoke.

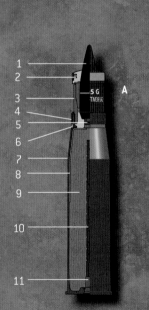
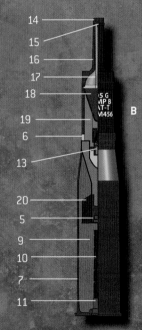
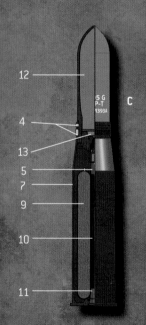
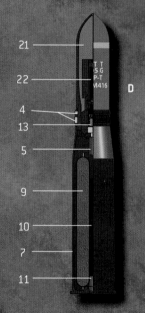

1. Sheathed core
2. Centring band
3. Sabot
4. Rotating band
5. Tracer
6. Obdurator
7. Cartridge case
8. Liner
9. Propellant
10. Igniter tube
11. Electric primer
12. Warhead explosive
13. BD fuze
14. Impact switch assembly
15. Piezoelectric power supply
16. Stand-off spike
17. Wire lead
18. Copper liner
19. Shaped charge
20. Fin and boom assembly
21. WP charge
22. Burster

Provides limited smoke screen from choice of two smoke grenade launchers or engine smoke generator (US Army 1980: 1-3)

Some of these points are worth exploring in terms of IDF experience. The water-fording ability was, in many cases, of little direct relevance to the arid battlefields of the Middle East. What was practical, however – and not quoted here – were the M60A1's abilities in handling trenches and obstacles. The tank was capable of a vertical-object climb of 1.24m and of crossing a ditch 2.74m wide. The points made about illumination, in the form of searchlights, do not seem directly applicable to the Magach 6/6A tanks used in 1973. None of the M60/M60A1 photographs seen by the author shows the tanks with the large over-barrel searchlight mounted (although I concede that such evidence might be out there).

The clash between Sagger and M60 in the Sinai Desert in 1973 was, in some ways, a David-and-Goliath type of encounter – the diminutive missile and its exposed operator fighting against a 51-tonne war machine. Yet the sheer number of Saggers, and – as we shall see – the tactical inexperience of the Israeli tank crews in fighting against anti-tank missiles, meant that in reality the outcome was in the balance. Both sides had technically sophisticated pieces of war-making equipment. What really mattered now was how they used them tactically and how well they adjusted to the unfolding battle.

M60/M60A1 AMMUNITION DISTRIBUTION AND ARMOUR PROTECTION

In the battle against the Sagger missile, the M60A1 tank crew had two chief forms of defence: first, their ability to put down rounds on the Sagger operator from the main gun and machine gun quickly during the missile's guided flight phase; second, the protection afforded by the tank's armour itself. The main-gun shells were stored in six different locations around the fighting compartment. Immediately to the left of the gunner was a three-round ready-rack magazine, plus another three rounds directly in front of him. The rest of the shells were distributed in larger racks, varying in number between 11 and 18 rounds, between the top left and the frontal sections of the fighting compartment. There were also several boxes of belted 7.62mm and .50-calibre machine-gun ammunition around the crowded inner space, plus ammunition for whatever small arms the crew might have taken on board (handguns and compact submachine guns such as the 9mm Uzi were popular). IDF tank crews actually adjusted their ammunition types according to the threat. Major-General Emanuel Sakal noted that in M48A3 (Magach 3) units the standard load was 24 APDS, 15 HEAT, 16 HEP, four white phosphorus (useful for blinding the Sagger operators) plus four fléchette shells, this last being a round that fired dozens of tiny arrows that served both to kill Sagger operators and also to cut the wires of Sagger missiles in flight.

The M60A1's armour was of the homogenous steel type, making it the last US-made tank to have such armour, before composite types took over. Naturally, this armour was thickest at the front of the hull and turret. The protection levels dropped to their thinnest on the sides, rear and top, varying from 140mm (turret side) down to 25mm (turret top), the latter being an indicator that the days of top-attack missiles had yet to arrive. Just as important as the physical depth of the armour was the angle at which the armour was presented to incoming fire. The greater the angle, the greater the actual depth of armour the shot had to pass through while at the same time dealing with shot deflection. The top front hull armour and front turret armour were 65 degrees and 72 degrees from the vertical, respectively.

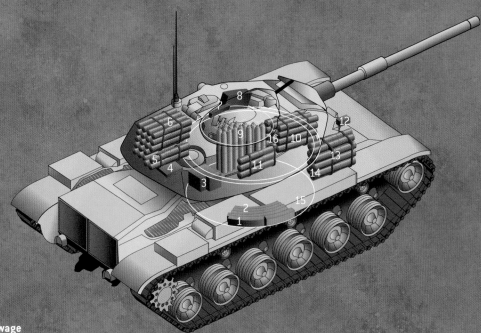

Ammunition stowage

1. 7.62mm ammunition boxes (3,750 rounds)
2. .50-calibre ammunition boxes (720 rounds)
3. Hand grenade box (eight grenades)
4. .45-calibre ammunition box (180 rounds)
5. 105mm ammunition tubular stowage rack (three rounds)
6. 105mm ammunition tubular stowage rack (18 rounds)
7. .50-calibre ready rounds ammunition box (180 rounds)
8. 7.62mm ready rounds ammunition box (2,200 rounds)
9. 105mm ammunition ready rack (13 rounds)
10. 105mm ammunition tubular stowage rack (15 rounds)
11. 105mm ammunition stowage tray (three rounds)
12. .45-calibre ammunition box (180 rounds)
13. 105mm ammunition tubular stowage rack (11 rounds)
14. Waist of turret ring (inner and outer edges)
15. Floor of turret ring
16. Commander's cupola ring

Armour depths/angle from vertical

a. 109mm/65°   c. 208mm/35°   e. 25–35mm/85°   g. 115mm/35°   i. 60mm/81°

b. 114mm/35°   d. 45mm/72°   f. 25mm/90°   h. 74mm/0°

THE COMBATANTS

The results of the Six-Day War were as much psychological and cultural as they were military and geographical. For Israel, the massive victories won in less than a week of fighting produced a super-charged confidence in the superiority of the IDF over their Arab counterparts. For the Israeli military leadership, the Arab advantage in sheer manpower now counted for almost nothing, as the 1967 war indicated that numerical superiority could not translate into battlefield dominance, by virtue of Israeli tactical élan and aggressive manoeuvre warfare. In the period between 1967 and 1973, Israel continued to train its forces hard for war to maintain their readiness, but many in the subsequent IDF leadership looked back on this time as one of complacency, relaxed in the assumption of automatic victory. For example, Major-General Emanuel Sakal noted that: 'In June 1973 Iron Ram war game, a nine-hour defensive battle "succeeded" in clearing the eastern bank [of the Suez Canal] of enemy forces, followed immediately by an Israeli attack and canal crossing. Smugness characterized the Israelis' summary of the exercise: "Two Israeli tanks companies sufficed to 'wipe out' an Egyptian division". The IDF clearly underestimated the Egyptian soldiers' (Sakal 2014: 84).

Yet there is no denying that the Arabs had suffered a crippling psychological blow as a result of the Six-Day War. Israel's opponents had experienced the utter demoralization of their combined forces, vastly stronger on paper than their opponents, being wiped out in short order, losing thousands of square kilometres of territory in the process. The soul-searching among the Arab leadership was deep and painful. There were many reasons for the failure: poor leadership; lack of tactical knowledge and initiative among lower ranks; unintelligent use of armour and air assets; inadequate logistics. Although it would take more than six years to remodel an army, in the case of the Egyptian forces Nasser and then Sadat set about attempting to create a force that could fight with the same professionalism and confidence as the IDF. Not least this applied to the Sagger anti-tank teams who would form the heart of the Egyptian defence.

EGYPTIAN FORCES

The five divisions of Egyptian troops – 200,000 men in total – that gathered on and around the Suez Canal in October 1973 were quantitatively superior to their IDF opponents across the water, but they had also made huge qualitative leaps since the debacles of 1967. Two main factors had improved the force. First, Egypt had invested very heavily not only in Soviet weapon systems and vehicles, but also in the doctrine that came with them. In short, the Egyptian forces began to professionalize for modern warfare. Second, the Egyptians undertook substantial amounts of pre-operational training.

The Soviet war doctrine is complex to describe, and if looked at across the board would take us well away from our focus on Sagger-vs-M60 combat. One area that is directly relevant to our analysis, however, is the focus on highly coordinated combined-arms warfare, made efficient both by a higher quality of military leadership and a devolved tactical initiative among the lower ranks (particularly junior officers and NCOs) that raised the operational intelligence of the whole army. Military historian Dani Asher describes the key shift of this modern way of tactical thinking:

> The modern age is characterized by the shift from individual arms, based on the skill and muscle of the individual soldier, to team-operated weapons. This change has dramatically raised the importance of organizing and strengthening military units. A large number of

The first ATGWs actually encountered by the IDF were the 3M6 *Shmel* (AT-1 'Snapper'), of the type shown here. Yet the IDF's experience and understanding of these weapons during the 1960s were extremely limited, and counter-ATGW tactics were not built into IDF armoured training as standard. (AirSeaLand Photos/ Cody Images)

officers and individual soldiers unite into a smoothly functioning team. Coordination among military units operating under wartime conditions can be achieved through effective leadership and discipline, as well as by raising the soldiers' level of political education. (Asher 2009: 64–65)

This shift from individual thinking – whether an individual officer or an individual unit – to inter-arms-team coordination is especially apparent in the Egyptian organization of their forces for the 1973 war, all expressed within the horizons of maximum effort for limited goals. We can see it in the coordinated programme for the amphibious assault across the Suez Canal, which involved special-forces units, engineers, infantry, boat squads, armour, artillery and air power working together to overcome the physical obstacles of the canal and its sandbanks, plus the military obstacles of the Bar-Lev Line; but we can also see it clearly in the way that the Saggers were integrated into the overall order of battle. At the express orders of Lieutenant-General Saad El Shazly, Chief of Staff of the Egyptian Armed Forces during the Yom Kippur War, the Sagger missiles held in rear depots were stripped out and pushed into the hands of the front-line units, to increase the levels of anti-tank capability there. Thus in addition to the hundreds of RPGs, plus recoilless rifles, anti-tank cannon and (in mechanized and armoured divisions) SU-100 tank destroyers, each division included 72 Sagger launchers, with a company of 12 launchers allocated to each brigade and 36 launchers within an anti-tank battalion (Asher 2009: 136). In addition, an infantry division would also have a supporting tank brigade that included six BRDM-2s with their six-missile Sagger launchers, plus 36 BMP-1s with single Sagger launchers mounted atop the hull. The Egyptians were going into battle with one of the most intensive anti-armour screens in history.

The Egyptian leadership was also aware that the Saggers and their two- or three-man teams had to be applied with coordinated intent if they were to achieve maximum defensive effect. Thus much thought was given to how the Saggers would be applied to build up the anti-armour defence cohesively. Initially, the first-wave soldiers would move across the Suez Canal with their RPG-7s, to establish an immediate and portable short-range anti-armour screen. Then, with the second wave, each battalion of troops would deploy a platoon of Saggers, before recoilless rifles then went across with the troops of the third wave. With the understanding that the expenditure of missiles would be high in the first few hours, the fourth wave of soldiers would also include ammunition resupply, in the form of another four Sagger missiles for each launcher, and each of the succeeding waves would bring with them more Saggers and more missile units 'for reinforcing the battalions and brigade reserves' (Asher 2009: 138). Vehicle-mounted Sagger units would begin crossing and supporting the action once pontoons and other effective bridging systems had been thrown across the Suez Canal, and a continual flow of Saggers and other ATGWs would serve to build up anti-tank reserve forces behind the immediate front line. Dan Asher leaves us in no doubt about the scale of the Sagger deployment:

Each division was provided with a massive quantity of Saggers – sometimes as many as 1,250 missiles for the first three days of the fighting (460 on the first day alone). Each launch team was allocated twenty missiles and each infantry division twenty-four

During an Egyptian Army parade in the early 1970s, a BMP-1 shows a single Sagger missile mounted on a forward launch rail. To use the Sagger from an armoured vehicle, the crew would have to keep their vehicle stationary during the missile's flight time, a position that put the BMP-1 in considerable danger from return fire. (AirSeaLand Photos/Cody Images)

carriages for toting them. Each carriage carried an additional eight missiles, which meant that each team could be reinforced with some of the carriage's 192 missiles (plus four additional ones), besides the two that the teams had with them at the outset. (Asher 2009: 139)

Sheer volume of firepower was not a guarantee of tactical success in itself, however. What was also required was the training to use that firepower intelligently. Here again the Egyptian forces invested wisely in the run-up to the Yom Kippur War. Training was conducted among every element of the Egyptian forces, the work focusing on combat-realistic drills plus flexible battlefield decision making. Possibly the best example of the pay-off from this training was the incredible logistical and technical feat of crossing the Suez Canal and of hydrographically engineering access points through the towering Israeli sand barriers on the other side. On a lesser scale, however, the Sagger teams also received investment. For several years before the war, they would 'deploy' from simulator vans to practise firing their missiles and tracking them to moving targets. Chaim Herzog, formerly a major general in the IDF and President of Israel (1983–93), notes:

Even later, when the Israeli and Egyptian armies were ranged one against the other in a war of attrition inside Egypt on the west bank of the Suez Canal, Israeli forces noted the

SAAD EL SHAZLY

A large measure of the credit for the initial success of the Egyptian offensive in Sinai must be given to Lieutenant-General Saad El Shazly, at the time Chief of Staff of the Egyptian Armed Forces (1971–73). Born on 1 April 1922 in the village of Shobratana on the Nile Delta, El Shazly joined the Royal Military Academy in 1939, subsequently gaining combat experience as a lieutenant serving with British Empire forces in the Western Desert during World War II. During the war, he proved himself to be a capable and level-headed leader of men, and after the end of the conflict in 1945 his rise was little short of meteoric. He was the founder and commander of the first paratroops battalion in Egypt (1955–59), and in 1960 led the first United Arab Forces in Congo, within a United Nations deployment. During the Six-Day War in 1967, El Shazly was one of few Egyptian commanders to emerge with his reputation intact, when he was Commander of the Special Forces Corps (Commandos & Paratroopers). His successful night extraction of a combined infantry and armour force earned him lasting respect in the Egyptian Army, and during 1970–71 he commanded the Third Field Army, with the rank of lieutenant-general. He became Chief of Staff of the Egyptian Armed Forces in May 1971, in which capacity he took the lead in developing Operation *Badr*. Despite the brilliance of this plan and the confidence of its execution, it was the Yom Kippur War that would prove the undoing of El Shazly's career. Having fallen out with President Anwar Sadat over the conduct and future strategy of the war, El Shazly was removed from his post, and shifted out to unobtrusive foreign ambassador roles. Later in the 1970s, his alienation from the Egyptian government increased with his criticism of the Camp David Agreement and the publication of his book *The Crossing of the Suez* (1980), for which he was court-martialled for divulging military secrets (a charge he vigorously denied). A long period of exile and a subsequent imprisonment followed, a shameful treatment of a man who was one of the few to have shown leadership and integrity during the 1973 conflict. El Shazly died on 10 February 2011, and after the January revolution in that year his name was restored to a position of honour within public life.

Lieutenant-General Saad El Shazly (left), depicted here next to President Anwar Sadat (centre) and Commander-in-Chief/Minister of War Ahmad Ismail Ali (right), was an unfortunate figure in modern Egyptian military history. (Universal History Archive/UIG via Getty Images)

simulator trucks driving up every day to undergo their daily anti-tank training. This system was repeated right down the line in the army until every action became a reflex action. (Herzog 2009: 35)

There is always the danger of making descriptions of battlefield deployments too 'clean', overlooking the sheer practical and logistical demands and the unpredictability of shifting tens of thousands of men and vehicles across a resistant battlespace. El Shazly was all too aware of these issues, right down to the needs of the individual soldier. One of the biggest headaches was how to give each soldier all he needed to survive and fight with reasonable independence, but without overloading him. Add a Sagger or other hefty weapon system, and you had a truly burdened warrior:

> First, survival needs. For 24 hours, plus a margin in case he hit trouble or got lost, each man would need five pounds of food and four and a half pints of water, a steel helmet, field kit and minimum clothing. Total: 25lbs. Margin for weaponry: 40lbs. That was ample for the standard infantryman. His rifle, 300 rounds and two grenades weigh about 35lbs. But what of those carrying portable support weapons? The list was formidable: ATGWs (Russian codename MALOTKA); SAM-7s (codename STRELLA); the 82mm mortar; our anti-tank guns; the 82mm and 107mm recoilless launchers (B-10 and B-11) and the rocket-propelled grenades (RPGs); the medium machine guns; the 12.7mm anti-aircraft machine guns; the flame-throwers, and on and one. Those were all very heavy. Their crews could never carry them plus the minimum ammunition they would need to face the counter-attacks we expected. The solution was to distribute the loads among groups of infantry men detailed to stick together as assault teams (which sounds easy until you try to ensure that each member of the team can still carry out individual tactical tasks). Even so, I did not succeed. When the final lists for each infantry division were drawn up, individual loads varied between 60lbs and 75lbs and, in a few cases, even heavier. (El Shazly 2003: 58–59)

Controlling weight build-up has been a perennial problem for leaders of all ages and wars. Given the need to establish an effective anti-tank barrier on the other side of the Suez Canal, it is difficult to see how the weight accretion could be controlled for Sagger troops. Yet El Shazly succeeded in fielding Sagger teams that were well-armed, well-trained and had clear objectives for the immediate future.

ISRAELI FORCES

It is difficult to identify which was the premier arm of service in the IDF by 1973, such was the standard of excellence across the forces. Israel boasted unsurpassed special forces and paratroopers, a regionally dominant air force, well-trained and self-disciplined infantry, and a small but excellent (and often overlooked) navy. If there were any particular arm at the heart of the land forces, however, it would arguably be the Israeli Armored Corps (IAC).

One of the most important figures of the IAC was Major-General Israel Tal, who took command of the Israeli armoured forces in 1964. Following Israel's Sinai campaign of 1956, and subsequent clashes with Syrian forces in the Golan Heights, Tal became utterly focused on the importance of making the IAC's armour and crews the best in the world. Tal had two main needs: improved armoured vehicles (and more of them) and better training for armour crews. The first was satisfied during the 1960s with a substantial programme of tank reconstruction and purchase, especially equipping Centurion and Sherman tanks with the new 105mm L7 main gun and improved powerplants, plus purchasing the M48A2 and upgrading it to M60 standard. The second consisted of a heavy investment in training, especially in the skills of

efficient and fast long-range gunnery, meticulous maintenance procedures and intelligent offensive action to overcome Arab numerical superiority.

The result of Tal's efforts, and that of the many capable men under him, was that the IAC became the superlative war-winning force that carved its way through Arab armour during the Six-Day War of 1967. The lesson appeared clear: offensive action was king. This lesson took a deep hold right through to the Yom Kippur War, and many have suggested that the overwhelming bias towards the offensive meant that the defensive measures and training put in place in the Sinai in the run-up to the Yom Kippur War were not adequate to meet the scale of the threat. Major-General Sakal observes, for example:

> In principle, the IDF combat doctrine assumed a balanced approach to battle, but in practice, more resources were always allocated to the offensive battle. A careful look at the 1973 training schedule reveals that of the twenty-eight main lessons planned for 252nd and 143rd Divisions, only one dealt with defense; for 146th and 210th Divisions training exercises, not a single defensive lesson was planned. Brigade exercises included one lesson in organizing a hasty defense (but this allotted time was usually frittered away). (Sakal 2014: 15)

This is not to say that Israeli armour crews went into battle in 1973 with insufficient training. Any tanker heading into action in 1973 would have started his career with 11 weeks of basic training, which gave him physical fitness, the essential skills of soldiering and the core understanding of armoured warfare and armoured vehicles. Then it was on to a full two months of specialized training at the Armored School, in which each recruit would be instilled with knowledge relating to one particular specialism: gunnery, loading, driving or communications. Once the men had passed this phase, they were put together with officers who had come out of the officers'

ABOVE LEFT
Two of the key Israeli figures of the Yom Kippur War. At right, on the very rear of the truck, is GOC Southern Command, Major-General Shmuel 'Gorodish' Gonen, conversing with the commander of the 143rd Reserve Armored Division, Major-General Ariel 'Arik' Sharon (the other bareheaded figure). The two men rarely worked together on favourable terms during the war. (AirSeaLand Photos/Cody Images)

ABOVE RIGHT
This Israeli tank crewman is holding an Armour-Piercing Discarding Sabot (APDS) shell, with the nose of the sub-calibre tungsten penetrator clearly visible with the sabot casing at the tip of the round. These munitions were almost exclusively used against other tanks or heavily armoured vehicles. (AirSeaLand Photos/Cody Images)

Israeli Centurion tanks conduct manoeuvres in the Negev Desert in February 1970. Most of the training conducted by IDF armour in the run-up to the Yom Kippur War focused on offensive action, assuming a clear superiority over Arab forces. This was one of the reasons why the IDF was ill-prepared for the professionalism of the Egyptian Army attack of 6 October 1973. (AirSeaLand Photos/Cody Images)

training and assembled into crews and assigned to tanks. Now they would conduct a further two months of field training, up to company-level manoeuvres. Even once they had passed through all the training phases, their skills were kept fresh through numerous war games and exercises conducted in the Sinai and Negev deserts. These exercises, however, generally worked around scenarios of an Arab assault being stopped rapidly (usually within a couple of hours), then repulsed by a vigorous Israeli counter-attack.

This training was certainly profitable, but during the Yom Kippur War several training gaps at the crew level were apparent. One directly related to the understanding of the Sagger, and of anti-tank defence in general. The influence of the Sagger certainly doesn't appear to have percolated through the IAC ranks to any great extent:

> The acquisition by the Egyptians and Syrians of the Sagger anti-tank missile made little impression on the Israelis. They had encountered a number of the missiles in exchanges of fire across the lines during the War of Attrition and regarded them as just another antitank weapon along with conventional antitank guns, recoilless rifles, and tanks themselves, not a threat that required a basic revision of doctrine. AMAN printed booklets about the Sagger's characteristics based on information received from the United States, which had encountered the missile in Vietnam in 1971. The armored corps command had even developed tactics for dealing with the missile. But neither the

ISRAEL TAL

Born in Machanayim, Palestine in 1924, Israel Tal would spend most of his life in uniform, in the process exerting a truly formative influence over the development and doctrine of the Israel Defense Forces (IDF). Having volunteered for British Army service at the age of 17, Tal, like many of his generation, learned about the reality of war fighting in the Western Desert and then in Italy. At the end of World War II he returned to Palestine and joined the Haganah paramilitary force, which with the establishment of the State of Israel in May 1948 became the foundation of the IDF, with Tal serving as a junior officer in its ranks. Over the next two decades, Tal emerged as an exceptional commander, distinguishing himself in the 1948 Arab-Israeli War and (as commander of the 10th Infantry Brigade) the 1956 Sinai campaign. His transfer to command of the Israeli Armored Corps (IAC) in 1964 gave him the chance to implement his 'pure tank' doctrine, placing armoured vehicles at the centre of IDF tactical and strategic direction. Tal held command of the IAC from 1964 to 1969, and during that time he also instilled excellence into the Armored School, dividing it into seven highly competent training wings: gunnery, signals, driving, maintenance, tactical, commanders and officers. There were also special training programmes for each different tank type in service. The training programmes he implemented made the IDF armour crews the best in the world, with exceptional skills in manoeuvre and long-range gunnery. The Six-Day War more than vindicated his approach, but the Yom Kippur War forced a reappraisal of how the doctrine needed adaptation for the ATGW era. The Yom Kippur War also brought Tal into conflict with his superiors, particularly over his (accurate) interpretation of pre-war intelligence and his refusal to keep fighting the Egyptian Third Army on the west bank of the

Israel Tal was a true believer in the power of armour and its centrality to IDF tactical success. The experience of encountering ATGWs en masse during the Yom Kippur War, however, placed a question mark over the authority of the tank, and that authority is still being debated and analysed to this day. (Israel Tal/CC BY-SA 3.0)

Suez after a ceasefire agreement. He retired from the Army in 1974, but as part of the Defense Ministry worked on designing what became the Merkava tank, still the core MBT of the IDF to this day. The Merkava is regarded worldwide as one of the finest tanks since 1945, and a powerful memorial to Tal, who died on 8 September 2010.

booklets nor the suggested tactics had yet filtered down and few tankmen were even aware of the Sagger's existence. (Rabinovich 2004: 35)

The lack of awareness of the Sagger is perhaps understandable, given that the missile had not entered the Middle Eastern war zones in earnest. It is commonplace for armies to train to fight the previous war, and to date the IAC had not had to wrestle with a broad and concentrated anti-tank defence. Two other comments from veterans of the IAC include: 'We were never told to expect and didn't train against missiles' and 'I was an instructor in the armor school just before the war and we were never taught to cope with missiles and infantry to any extent' (quoted in Atwater 1991: 26).

What the IAC did have in abundance, however, was experience. Many, if not most, of the commanders who stood in the turrets of IAC tanks had first-hand combat experience, in some cases stretching back over a decade. Ehud Gross was one such individual, and he gives an interesting insight into both the martial knowledge of armour crews and their impressions of the M60A1:

> At the beginning of the war on October 6, 1973, I was a young major in the education department of the IDF. I had no assigned mobilisation role in a combat unit, but I had a lot of experience in tanks and commanding, starting with the battles for the water sources against the Syrians in 1965, then as a tank platoon commander in the 1967 war in battles against the Jordanians and the battles on the Golan Heights against the Syrians. At the start of the 1973 war, I called the Armor Corps headquarters looking for a free unit of tanks to participate in. First I was sent to the 421st Armored Brigade as a battalion commander, but the original deputy commander who I was supposed to replace showed up, so I was sent to the 407th Tank Battalion of the 600th Armored Brigade as a company commander. I was assigned to command A Company. I had experience on various versions of the Sherman, M48 Patton, and then the upgraded M48A3/Magach 3, so I knew armour. I was very impressed with the M60A1 which I now commanded. It was fast, stable, roomy, reliable, and quite well-equipped (except for no night sights!) and had a large supply of rounds for its 105mm cannon. I had to study quickly to understand all of the capabilities of this new tank. At the start of the war, we were engaged in defensive battles with high mobility in the central zone area of the Sinai. (Quoted in Nordeen & Isby 2010: 23)

By 1973 Gross had six years of combat experience, plus the additional training and field exercise that inevitably accompany the life of a soldier. What is important is the slight urgency with which Gross had to accustom himself to his new mount. As noted previously, 150 new M60A1 tanks were delivered to Israel in 1971, entering service with the 600th Armored Brigade and 87th Armored Reconnaissance Battalion. Colonel Tuvia Raviv remembered the acquisition of the new vehicles, which in some cases seem largely to have just rolled off the production lines:

> I was appointed the commander of the 600th Armored Brigade in September 1971 when the brigade did not exist. I guess I got the job as a result of my considerable armour experience ... I had to establish the 600th Armored Brigade from nothing and for that mission I got experienced tank veterans from the [1969–70] static war and new M60A1 tanks which were not equipped with all of the required systems, such as no machine guns etc. My brigade finished training just weeks before the 1973 war. (Quoted in Nordeen & Isby 2010: 21)

It is apparent that the training programmes for the M60A1s were only just implemented prior to the outbreak of war in October 1973. Added to the lack of awareness of Sagger capabilities, it is not inconceivable that the lack of familiarity with the M60A1 – particularly among commanders – might have contributed to some of

the heavy casualties among the type during the Yom Kippur War. Yehuda Geller was another unit leader in the 600th Armored Brigade, and this sense of inexperience with the M60A1 is evident in the following quotation:

> I completed my basic training in the late 1960s using the Sherman M50 and the French AMX13 light battle tanks, and served my reserve duty from 1961 to 1973 as the commander of patrol units of the reserve and regular Armored Corps ... The 600th Brigade was equipped with 111 M60A1 tanks according to the IDF standard, in three battalions: 409th, 407th, and 410th. Each battalion included 36 tanks plus three at the brigade headquarters ... Following my initiative and the injury to both [previous] commanders of the 410th Battalion of the 600th Brigade … I was appointed as commander of the 410th Battalion on the third day of the Yom Kippur War; and that was the first time I mounted the IDF Patton tank. My personal experience regarding the technological aspects of the M60 was very limited … (Quoted in Nordeen & Isby 2010: 21 & 26)

So it was that the Yom Kippur War brought together two armies, both well trained and both containing a high degree of experience. Yet in the case of the clash between the M60 and the Sagger, the steepest learning curve, at least initially, would be experienced by the crews of the former.

One important point to note about the following narrative is that it purely focuses on the Sinai campaign. This is for the simple reason that M60s were not used on the Golan Heights, as it was felt that their American track systems would not be suited to the terrain in that theatre. As it was, the Golan Heights told its own story of the Sagger-vs-armour saga, but in that case the IDF tanks were principally Centurions and Super Shermans.

In front of an audience that includes Israeli Prime Minister Golda Meir and (with defining eyepatch) Minister of Defense Moshe Dayan, Major-General Avraham 'Bren' Adan (commander of the Israeli Armored Corps) delivers a briefing. (AirSeaLand Photos/Cody Images)

COMBAT

While Israeli intelligence largely predicted that it would be 1975 before the Arabs were able to launch a general offensive, President Sadat was aiming for October 1973. In the immediate run-up to the attack, many in the IDF did become sensitized to the signs, so that the 252nd Armored Division – the principal armoured reserve force in the Sinai – did raise its level of alert, but requests for reinforcements were initially turned down. The belief was that Israeli forces would have at least a full 48 hours' warning of an offensive, such was the confidence in the intelligence. As the hour of attack approached, the intelligence was updated, to the extent that early on 6 October Major-General Eli Zeira, of the Israeli Military Intelligence Directorate, told Minister of Defense Moshe Dayan, Chief of Staff of the IDF General David 'Dado' Elazar, and General Israel Tal that the onslaught would indeed begin that day, but around sunset. The moves for mobilization were upgraded, but disagreements over its extent and the belief that that attack would come at sunset meant that when the Egyptian offensive did begin, it achieved a significant measure of tactical surprise.

The Egyptian attack against the IDF in Sinai began at 1400hrs on 6 October, with an air attack by 240 Arab fighters and ground-attack aircraft against Israeli SAM batteries, command posts and other key targets. Simultaneously, 2,000 artillery pieces opened up with rippling fire on the 15 *Maozim* strongpoints of the Bar-Lev Line, which shuddered upon the impact of some 175 shells per second – 10,500 rounds were fired during the first minute alone of the 53-minute bombardment. At 1415hrs, the actual Suez Canal crossing began. Here, the Egyptian investment in training and engineering paid off spectacularly. Utilizing some 790 small boats (of the 2,500 craft used in total across the front), some 4,000 men passed over the river north of the Great Bitter Lake, clambered over the sand ramparts, and either attacked Israeli strongpoints and command posts, or worked to set up anti-tank positions in expectation of the

IDF infantry hunker down in rapidly excavated desert foxholes. The infantry would play a central part in the evolving countermeasures against the Sagger threat, especially when deployed by APCs specifically to hunt down Sagger teams, who betrayed their position during the missile's visible flight. (AirSeaLand Photos/Cody Images)

certain IDF armoured response. Around the Great Bitter Lake itself (which did not have a sand rampart), the Egyptian 130th Amphibious Brigade made its own crossing, with significant amounts of armour. Casualties during the initial assault crossing totalled just 208 men, a fraction of the 30,000 that had been predicted.

These initial crossings were just the tip of the spear. Engineers across the front used high-pressure hoses to cut passages through the protective sandbanks on the eastern bank of the Suez Canal, through which armour would ultimately pass, and roughly every 15 minutes another wave of infantry were transported across the Suez Canal to develop and expand the five bridgeheads that had been established. By 1630hrs, just under 24,000 Egyptian soldiers had been deployed and were in action in the eastern Sinai. Bridging units were already hard at work by this point, as were the crews of huge amphibious rafts that carried across four tanks at a time. By 2200hrs, the infrastructure was in place for entire divisions and armoured brigades to cross the Suez Canal (500 tanks crossed on the night of 6/7 October). With the Egyptian Second Army traversing between the Great Bitter Lake and the Mediterranean Sea, and the Third Army between the Great Bitter Lake and the Gulf of Suez, the Israelis had to invoke a massive counter-response to stabilize the threat.

INITIAL CLASHES

As well as being emplaced in large numbers on the west bank of the Suez Canal, the Sagger teams were also at the forefront of the crossing operation. The ATGW units worked quickly to dig shallow trenches for the missile operator, often sandbagging the parapets to protect against the small-arms and mortar fire that in many ways posed the greatest threat to the exposed teams. Up to 15m away from these trenches, the missiles were set up on their suitcase launchers, the nose cones oriented to the predicted avenues of attack from Israeli armour. Specifically, the Sagger units were targeting the prepared tank firing ramps by the sides of the *Maozim* strongpoints. Under the blazing heat of the afternoon sun, they readied themselves for the attackers.

A rare image of a Sagger operator in the Sinai, October 1973, preparing to launch his missile. The fact that the missile could be up to 15m away from the operator assisted in the operator's survival, as it made it harder for the enemy to pinpoint his exact position for delivering return fire. (Egyptian Government Information Office)

On the IDF side, for a time confusion and shock reigned. Operation *Shovach Yonim* (Dovecote) – the IDF plan for a counter-strike against just such a crossing of the Suez Canal – was initiated by Southern Command, the immediate tool of which was the 252nd Armored Division under Major-General Avraham Albert Mandler. This consisted of the 14th, 401st and 460th Armored brigades. Finding accurate source information for the IDF Order of Battle in the Sinai campaign is difficult, with apparently equally authoritative sources often not agreeing on the type of armour deployed with each IDF brigade. The 401st Armored Brigade in particular, led by Colonel Dan Shomron, is variously given as composed of either Magach 3s (M48A3s) or Magach 6s (M60s). The most likely scenario is that the brigade had either the first iteration of the M60 tank and/or M48A3s upgraded with the 105mm L7 main gun and the diesel powerplant used in the M60. Either way, they fall within the limit of our study here.

The immediate priority was to rush the brigades of the 252nd Armored Division up to the front line, to attempt to stop the expansion of the Egyptian bridgeheads and to bolster the crumbling defence of the *Maozim* strongpoints. In the northern part of the front, the Centurions and M48s of the 460th Armored Brigade pushed in the direction of El Qantara, while the central part of the front, around Lake Timsah, was the responsibility of the 14th Armored Brigade. In the south, between the Little Bitter Lake and the Gulf of Suez, the tanks of the 401st Armored Brigade moved into action.

Although the IDF had been taken by surprise, confidence was largely high among the Israeli armour crews, who felt more assured that they could dictate the pace of events now that they were on the offensive; but largely deployed in small, vulnerable units, they were about to come into contact with the Saggers. A US Army analysis of the Yom Kippur War, produced in 1975, quoted one of the armour crews' experience of these weapons in the first days of combat:

We were advancing and in the distance I saw specks dotted on the sand dunes. I couldn't make out what they were. As we got closer, I thought they looked like tree stumps. They

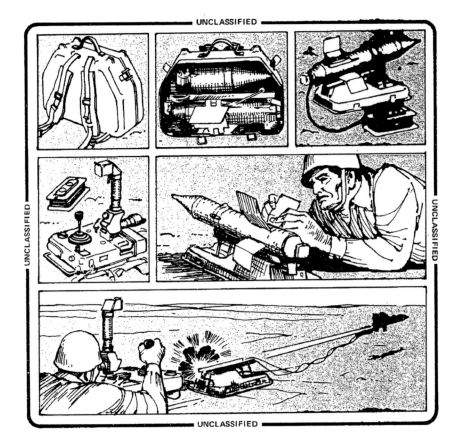

A US Army Training and Doctrine Command (TRADOC) cartoon strip illustrates the components and set-up of the AT-3 Sagger. Note the wires coming out the back of the missile in the last frame. Such wires curled around a burnt-out tank were a strong indicator of a Sagger strike. (US TRADOC)

were motionless and scattered across the terrain ahead of us. I got on the intercom and asked the tanks ahead what they made of it. One of my tank commanders radioed back: 'My God, they're not tree stumps. They're men!' For a moment I couldn't understand. What were men doing standing out there – quite still – when we were advancing in our tanks towards them? Suddenly all hell broke loose. A barrage of missiles was being fired at us. Many of our tanks were hit. We had never come up against anything like this before ... (Quoted in US TRADOC 1975: 18)

Apparent in this account is the shock of the new, as the crews adjusted to several unusual factors: the low profile of the Sagger (and RPG) operators in the desert; the sheer number of them 'scattered across the terrain'; and the shocking impact and accuracy of the missiles against the armour. Other observations from IDF tank crews mentioned that obscuration caused by dust was a significant issue; while a commander standing in his turret, or looking through vision blocks, can maintain visual contact with an MBT even at distance and through dust, observing a single human figure at distances of more than 1km through sand-impregnated air was a challenge. Note also that if the operator was well dug in, nothing more than the 9Sh16 periscope sight might be above ground to indicate the operator, with a profile no greater than a large branch. In many cases, the initial countermeasure was simply to loose off several shells in the general direction of the ATGW teams.

SAGGER TARGET VIEW

A 9M14M missile snakes out from its launcher towards a distant IDF M60A1 tank on 6 October 1973. We are looking at the target through the 9Sh16 periscope sight. To guide the missile onto the target, the operator has to keep the centre of the periscope reticle on the target, while simultaneously using the joystick of the 9S415 control unit to 'fly' the missile onto the same aim point. To guide his efforts, the red sighting flare on the side of the missile body burns throughout the flight (up to the Sagger's 3km range), but the abrupt flight characteristics of the missile mean that visually the flare bobs and weaves across the landscape, and requires smooth joystick corrections to maintain track on target. In the second of these images, the missile has just struck the tank, producing a cloud of smoke as the tank begins to brew up inside. Rather than deliver an instantly heavy destructive punch like a tank shell, the Sagger missile would typically burn a fist-sized hole through the armour, inflicting severe wounds on those inside through the effects of 'spall' and the scorching jet of metal steel, which would also ignite ammunition and fuel.

On the other side, there was an air of familiarity for the Sagger operators in these opening engagements. During the weeks before the offensive, each operator might have been involved in 20–30 firing simulations daily, and indeed a Sagger operator could have fired a total of 2,300 simulations just to qualify. The experiences of one soldier in charge of a Sagger team, Abdul Alati, attest to the competence and concentrated aggression of the Sagger teams. In the space of just ten minutes, Alati claimed no fewer than eight Israeli tanks. He remembered: 'The tanks accelerated to their maximum to avoid our rockets, but we could hit them in their weakest spots as long as they remained in range. Every Egyptian missile was worth an Israeli tank' (quoted in Atwater 1991: 27). One Israeli armour officer, Lieutenant Yuval Neria, who led an M48 tank company (K Company) in the 79th Battalion, had other memories of the horror and confusion of being under Sagger attack: 'It was a muddy area, a marsh. The people reacting to the missiles were trying to maneuver, trying to

M60A1 TARGET VIEW

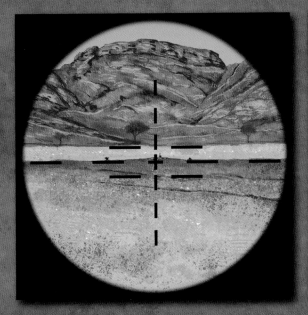
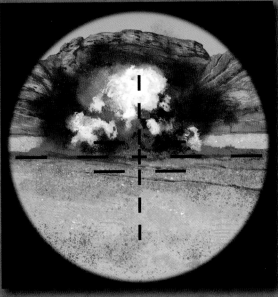

In the southern sector of the Sinai Front on 6 October 1973, the gunner of an IDF M60A1 spots and destroys an Egyptian Sagger team as they prepare to launch their missile at the Israeli armour from a distance of around 800m. The view here is through the reticle of an M32 periscope for the 105mm main gun. The aiming cross in the centre is bracketed by vertical mil lines to assist with the quick calculation of elevation or depression of the gun barrel, while the lines extending out horizontally either side are lead lines for calculating the right lead to apply to moving targets. In this case the target is static, and consists of three elements: in the centre, the Sagger operator, looking through the 9Sh16 periscope sight attached to a 9S415 joystick control; to the left, the Sagger missile itself sitting ready on its launcher rail; and to the right, another member of the Sagger team, observing the intended target through binoculars. Having spotted the Sagger, the commander quickly has the gunner put down a HESH shell onto the position, obliterating it before the Sagger operator has time to launch and guide the missile to target.

escape them, to confuse the missile launchers by zigzagging. Half an hour after we arrived in the area, we were more or less finished as a company' (quoted in Atwater 1991: 27).

At the beginning of the battle, Neria's company had possessed 11 tanks, but after the predations of the Sagger teams only his tank and one other were operational on the battlefield. The tactical imbalance between one Sagger control-unit operator and eight MBTs destroyed is profound. Such were the number of targets presenting themselves that the Sagger operator might find he was switching between three of four connected missiles in quick succession. In terms of optimal range, the Sagger crews also gained some useful information, finding that the best range for engagement was between 1,000m and 2,000m.

For the M60s of the 401st Armored Brigade, their first afternoon of fighting against the enemy was as harrowing as that of their comrades further north. They not only had to face the Saggers, which had deployed in significant numbers, but they also had to cope with numerous other threats – RPG-7s, enemy armour (often outnumbering the Israeli tanks), artillery fire, anti-tank cannon and recoilless rifles. Although precise figures of the losses sustained are not available, they were certainly a significant portion of the 153 tanks the 252nd Armored Division lost between 1400hrs on 6 October and daybreak on 7 October. In fact, by 0800hrs on 7 October, only 23 of Shomron's tanks were still operable.

THE ISRAELI RESPONSE

As the Sinai offensive entered its second day, it was clear that the Egyptians had much cause for celebration. In 24 hours not only had they advanced two armies across the Suez Canal, amounting to 100,000 men, 1,020 tanks and 3,500 other vehicles, they had also surrounded the Bar-Lev Line (the individual outposts were starting to fall), inflicted heavy losses on the IAF through establishing a dense and sophisticated SAM defence and, in large measure thanks to the Saggers, had blunted initial IDF armoured counter-attacks. Israeli tanks continued to be destroyed at an alarming rate – the 252nd Armored Division had just 100 tanks in action by the end of the morning of 7 October. What was clear to both sides, however, was that the IDF would pull in its armoured reserves and its mobilized infantry forces and would, at some point soon, launch a counter-attack. El Shazly noted that in effect a race was on:

> For both sides, Sunday [7 October] was a race to prepare for that big battle. The very success of our deception operation had handed the enemy some advantages in this race. The principal benefit was that our deployments were fully revealed: the five sectors; the heavily reinforced infantry divisions in each; our tactics at the perimeters; the caution of our steady moves forward; the nature, density and effectiveness of our portable SAM and ATGW. The enemy could plan their counter-attack on fairly full knowledge. Had their reserves been available in the later stages of our initial assault, by contrast, they would have attacked in considerable ignorance of our plans and of what our infantry could achieve. (El Shazly 2003: 233)

Gonen was rushing reinforcements into the Sinai, in the form of Ugda *Bren* (162nd Reserve Armored Division; Major-General Avraham 'Bren' Adan), Ugda *Arik* (143rd Reserve Armored Division; Major-General Ariel 'Arik' Sharon) and Ugda *Kalman* (146th Reserve Armored Division; Brigadier-General Kalman Magen). The force included most of the IDFs stocks of M60A1s, contained principally within the 600th Reserve Armored Brigade (Colonel Tuvia Raviv) and the 87th Armored Reconnaissance Battalion, adding another 23 M60A1s to Ugda *Arik*.

A plan was developed by Gonen and Elazar for an armour-led counter-attack. In broad outline, the plan involved Ugda *Bren* attacking in a north–south direction from around El Qantara parallel to the Suez Canal, and about 3km inland, sweeping up the Egyptian bridgehead in an aggressive flanking attack. Meanwhile, Ugda *Arik* would

Some half of all the fatalities incurred by the IDF during the Yom Kippur War were sustained by armoured vehicle crews, particularly those in tanks. Injuries caused by Sagger impacts included severe burns and fragmentation injuries caused by spalling and penetration through the armour. (AirSeaLand Photos/Cody Images)

be held further south around Tasa. The intention for Sharon's division was that it would, if Ugda *Bren*'s attack seemed to be developing successfully, make its own counter-attack against the Third Army below the Great Bitter Lake. If Bren's attack did not appear to be succeeding, however, then Sharon's division would move in to support. The 87th Armored Reconnaissance Battalion, meanwhile, was detached from the 143rd Reserve Armored Division and was positioned at Hamadia, a sandy hill overlooking a point on the Suez Canal that had been designated for a future Israeli crossing.

The Israeli plan had several flaws from the outset. First, it overestimated how much IDF offensive brilliance could achieve against a well-emplaced, massive and broadly armed Egyptian force. Second, it failed to address the fact that although the movement of the counter-attack was north–south, at some point the armoured drive would need to turn in and attack west, which would bring it within the range and capabilities of the Sagger teams and of the Egyptian tank gunners. Third, it had no significant artillery or air support – the armour would largely be on its own. Finally, the offensive was seriously weakened by detaching Sharon's division and sending it south – in effect, there would be no one to protect Adan's left flank. (Sharon was vigorously opposed to the plan from the start.) It should also be noted that all of the reserve divisions deployed had insufficient tank transporters, and therefore the combat vehicles drove across the entire Sinai Desert on their own tracks. Such an arduous movement had a severe wearing effect on the tanks' critical components, such as the tracks, suspension, transmission, engine filters and powerplant. It was also to the detriment of the crews themselves, who went into battle already feeling physically fatigued from a long journey in a hot, deafening and cramped MBT.

The first Israeli counter-attack in the Sinai was launched on the morning of 8 October. For Gonen and his staff at the Southern Command headquarters, confusion over battlefield reports led them, at least temporarily, to think that the push was going well, which prompted the decision to send Sharon's division south towards the Third Army. In fact, it was spiralling down into disaster. The 162nd Reserve Armored Division was lashed by repeated Sagger and RPG ambushes, plus tank fire from hundreds of Egyptian T-55s and T-62s. At 1200hrs, Adan radioed Gonen and reported: 'We have taken a lot of casualties, a great many. Tanks are burning from missiles' (quoted in Dunstan 2003: 56). The sombre tone about casualties was warranted. In one ambush alone, the 217th Reserve Armored Brigade lost 18 tanks within a matter of minutes, escaping from the carnage with just four tanks left.

Also under attack that day were the M60A1s of the 87th Armored Reconnaissance Battalion, which in its lonely position had come under the attentions of Arab anti-tank and artillery fire. It sustained many casualties, including the wounding of its CO, Lieutenant-Colonel Ben-Zion 'Bentzi' Carmeli. Eventually, as news of the Israeli collapse further north came in, the 600th Reserve Armored Brigade was recalled to the central part of the front, picking up the 87th Armored Reconnaissance Battalion along the way. Sharon's division had essentially spent a fruitless day driving around the Sinai.

ISRAELI RECOVERY

The failure of the attack of 8 October was a low point both for the IAC armour crews and for the IDF high command. Relations between the cautious Gonen and the belligerent Sharon degenerated to new lows, so much so that at one point Gonen asked Elazar to relieve Sharon of his command, a request that was resisted. It must also be remembered that the IDF was now fighting a two-front war, with intensive action on the Golan Heights. The IDF commanders realized that they did not have the strength to conduct an immediate and generalized offensive to reclaim Sinai and cross the Suez Canal. For now, they simply had to contain the Egyptian bridgeheads.

Major-General Gonen communicates with his field commanders via radio on 10 October 1973. On this date, the IDF was still largely on the back foot in the campaign, although the 1st Egyptian Infantry Brigade was destroyed when it moved out from under its SAM umbrella, a victory that boosted Israeli morale. (AirSeaLand Photos/Cody Images)

An Israeli M60 (right) sits next to an Egyptian T-54/T-55, the two destroyed within metres of one another during the battles around the Suez Canal. Note the extremely flat nature of the terrain around them, perfect for tank gunnery and ATGW tracking. (AirSeaLand Photos/Cody Images)

Yet unknown to the IDF commanders, strategic decisions made by the Egyptians would nudge the strategic and tactical advantage inch-by-inch back in Israel's favour. Encouraged by the initial successes, many in the Egyptian political and military leadership were advocating going beyond the original brief of limited gains, and were stoking more expansive ambitions for reclaiming territory. This was not a good move. The IDF might have appeared to have been on the back foot, but it was regaining its strength, and localized Arab armoured attacks – which often moved out beyond the protective range of the Sagger units – had been very roughly handled by the IDF tankers, who had superior skills in long-range gunnery. Furthermore, advancing far out into the Sinai would mean that Arab tanks would move from under the shade of the SAM umbrella into the harsh direct light of IAF ground-attack aircraft.

El Shazly came under pressure to make a bold new attack out into the Sinai to capture the strategically important Khatmia, Mitla and Gidi passes, gateways to the western Sinai. He resisted with passion, correctly judging that such drives would only serve to play to IDF strengths. Yet once President Sadat and his Commander-in-Chief/Minister of War, General Ahmad Ismail Ali, were united behind the new offensive, the die was cast – El Shazly received his orders on 12 October for an offensive two days later.

Bowing to the inevitable, El Shazly began to pull reserve armoured formations across the canal to reinforce the attack, which was scheduled for 14 October. As the units were deployed, it became clear to the Israelis that they were about to face a new offensive, but this time they would be ready, in both strength and attitude, to counter it. The IAC would serve to stop the Egyptian force dead, which it was confident of doing, both through its training and its superiority in number of tanks (Southern Command now had about 1,000 tanks compared to the 400 in the forthcoming Egyptian offensive). Once the Egyptian juggernaut's wheels were spinning in the sand and had lost traction, it could be taken apart by the IAF.

Meanwhile, the fighting went on around the *Maozim*, some further strongholds being lost to the Arabs after heroic resistance. One noteworthy Sagger victim was Major-General Mandler. On 13 October, he had been on the battlefield near the Mezach strongpoint, guiding operations from his M113 mobile command post. Unknown to him or his crew, an Egyptian Sagger team had spotted their vehicle and

This photograph shows a large force of Israeli M60A1s, likely to be of the 600th Reserve Armored Brigade (which contained the bulk of the IDF's Magach 6As), moving up to the Suez Canal to engage with Egyptian forces. (AirSeaLand Photos/Cody Images)

accurately launched a missile straight into the M113, whose armour was in no way adequate enough to stop the penetration and catastrophic destruction. Mandler was killed (he died while actually on the radio to Gonen), a bitter loss of a talented officer. Mandler's 252nd Reserve Armored Division was taken over by Major-General Kalman Magen, and the name changed to Ugda *Kalman*. (The previous Ugda *Kalman* thereafter became Ugda *Sassoon*.)

In terms of M60 and M60A1 dispositions for the attack, the tanks of the 600th Reserve Armored Brigade were positioned in the centre of the front, just above the Great Bitter Lake around Tasa, part of Sharon's Ugda *Arik*. The 87th Armored Reconnaissance Battalion had been assigned to the command of the 14th Reserve Armored Brigade, also part of Ugda *Arik* but which had been transferred from Ugda *Albert*. From 9 October, the 87th Armored Reconnaissance Battalion had been on an independent scouting mission, observing the boundary areas between the Second and Third armies and tasked with identifying weak points in the Egyptian defences that could be targeted for a subsequent Suez Canal crossing. The 401st Reserve Armored Brigade (now part of Ugda *Kalman*), meanwhile, was in the southern sector of the front, with its fellow divisional brigades attacking as a blocking force east of the land between the Little Bitter Lake and the Gulf of Suez.

The Egyptian offensive began at 1600hrs on 14 October. It was an unmitigated disaster for the Arab forces. Outgunned, outmanoeuvred and exposed to air attack, in just two hours 260 of the 400 tanks committed were destroyed, a good number of them falling victim to M60/M60A1 gunners.

For the Israelis, confidence and adrenaline now surged again. Furthermore, they were getting the measure of the Sagger, to some degree. First, during the offensive of 14 October, the Egyptians attempted to forward-deploy their Sagger teams in APCs and missile-equipped IFVs. Many of these were wrecked by Israeli tank fire before they could even deploy their missiles. In addition, the Israelis had devised new tactics for

An M48A3 crosses the Suez Canal during the later stages of the Yom Kippur War. The M48A3 had largely the same capabilities as the M60 when it was upgraded with the 105mm L7 main gun and the more powerful diesel engine used on the M60. (AirSeaLand Photos/Cody Images)

tackling the infantry Sagger teams, not least by taking evasive manoeuvres. Historian Abraham Rabinovich quotes the explanation of an operations officer of the 14th Armored Brigade (commanded by Colonel Amnon Reshef):

> Reshef's operations officer, Lt. Pinhas Bar ... assembled the tank commanders and explained the techniques developed in the past few hours for coping with the Sagger. Such impromptu lessons would be going on all along the front as new units took the field alongside tankers who had survived the day. The Saggers, the 'veterans' explained, were a formidable danger but not an ultimate weapon. They could be seen in flight and were slow enough to dodge. It took at least 10 seconds for a missile to complete its flight – at extreme range it could be twice that – during which time the Sagger operator had to keep the target in his sights as he guided the missile by the bright red light on its tail. From the side it was easy for the tankers to see the light. As soon as anyone shouted 'Missile,' the tanks were to begin moving back and forth in order not to present a stationary target. Movement would also throw up dust that would cloud the Sagger operator's view. Simultaneously, the tank should fire in his presumed direction, which itself could be sufficient throw off his aim. (Quoted in Rabinovich 2004: 111)

This evasive/offensive tactic for dealing with the Sagger became known as 'Sagger Watch', and proved to be effective. Despite the confidence of the Sagger teams, there was no doubt that a violently swerving target was not an easy one to hit over thousands of metres of distance, even with the Sagger guidance system and the operator's training. Add return fire from the M60s – each of which could fire one high-velocity shell every 6 seconds – and the operational environment for the Sagger teams was becoming ever more perilous.

The IDF was implementing other aggressive techniques to destroy the Sagger teams. An M113 APC or M3 half-track was attached to each pair of tanks, containing a squad of infantry plus its own heavy machine guns. At the moment the tanks were engaged, the infantry armour would identify the launch point and then race towards it, firing its machine guns on the move and, when in range, deploying the accompanying infantry to take out the Sagger team. The efficacy of these defensive tactics would be tested in no small measure when the IDF returned to the offensive.

OPERATION *GAZELLE* AND THE BATTLE OF CHINESE FARM

The focus of Israeli operations was now on launching a counter-offensive, crossing the Suez Canal, and forcing an Egyptian capitulation. At the centre of the operations supporting the crossing – codenamed Operation *Gazelle* – would be IDF M60s, as Raviv's 600th Reserve Armored Brigade and the 87th Armored Reconnaissance Battalion (still attached to the 14th Armored Brigade) would be in the vanguard. The plan was complex, but in summary broke down as follows. First, Sharon's division, Ugda *Arik*, was to attack and establish a bridgehead on the Suez Canal at Deversoir, while also clearing the metalled 'Akavish' and 'Tirtur' approach roads, which would be used to bring up reinforcements and bridge-crossing units and equipment (including a massive 180m-long prefabricated roller bridge, weighing *c.*400 tonnes and towed by 14 tanks). The attached 247th Reserve Paratroop Brigade would take and hold bridging and rafting locations. Second, once Ugda *Arik* had secured the bridgehead, the crossing would be developed and other armoured divisions (Ugda *Kalman* and Ugda *Bren*) would pour across and divide, making attacks both to the north and to the south, enveloping the Egyptian forces from the rear and threatening a deep push into Cairo itself.

The IDF operation to cross the Suez Canal was known variously as Operation *Abirey-Halev* or Operation *Abirey-lev*, and in English as Operation *Stout Heart* and Operation *Gazelle*. One of its by-products would be the most intense clash between Saggers and M60s of the war. The Egyptians, recognizing the importance of the area, just at the northern tip of the Great Bitter Lake (which acted as flank protection for both sides), had put in place heavy defensive positions including dozens of Sagger

Evidence of the intensity of the fighting: an Israeli M60A1 (centre) lies wrecked amid the steel corpses of other M60s on the banks of the Suez Canal. The Sagger, ATGW and armour threat remained high for IDF tank crews right up to the final moments of battle prior to the ceasefire on 25 October. (AirSeaLand Photos/ Cody Images)

An Israeli 105mm main gun, belonging to either an M60, a Centurion or an upgraded M48, fires on Egyptian positions around the Great Bitter Lake. IDF tank crews discovered that one solution to the Sagger problem was to hang back and pound the enemy positions with gunfire at long range. (AirSeaLand Photos/ Cody Images)

emplacements, especially around the crossroads of the Tirtur–Lexicon roads. Another bulwark against the IDF was 'Chinese Farm', a former Japanese agricultural research centre consisting of several low-rise buildings and a surrounding area laced with deep irrigation ditches, but now headquarters for both the Egyptian 21st Armoured and 16th Infantry divisions. Within these ditches – their fighting positions effectively already dug for them – were numerous prepared Sagger units, their missiles fanned out in a lethal 'hedgehog' of missile weaponry. In addition, the whole area was occupied by infantry, armour (dug-in Egyptian armour was one of the greatest threats to the Israelis), mortars and artillery. Taking it was not going to be an easy task for the IDF armour.

Operation *Gazelle* was a complex action, but here our focus will remain upon those portions of the battlefield involving the clash between M60s and Saggers. The opening elements of action, launched at 1500hrs on 15 October, saw the M60A1s of the 600th Reserve Armored Brigade making a diversionary attack against the Egyptian 16th Infantry Division along the Tasa–Ismailia road. This distracted the Egyptians from the critical thrust by Reshef's 14th Armored Brigade, still supported by the M60A1s of the 87th Armored Reconnaissance Battalion. This combined force was tasked with smashing through the tough Egyptian defences on the Akavish and Tirtur roads, clearing the roads in the process for follow-up troops, eliminating the enemy stronghold of Chinese Farm, and establishing a 5km-wide bridgehead on the bank of the Suez Canal. The 87th Armored Reconnaissance Battalion's main role was to move quickly to the canal crossing position and secure it for the 247th Reserve Paratroop Brigade.

For the soldiers of the 87th Armored Reconnaissance Battalion, the action began promisingly; they reached their main positions relatively unharmed, the Egyptians having been caught by surprise. This had not been the case for the 14th Armored Brigade's 18th Battalion and 40th Battalion. At the Tirtur–Lexicon crossroads, well-defended in themselves and overlooked by Chinese Farm, a massacre of IDF armour

took place. More than two companies of tanks were destroyed, many through the interlocking fire of dozens of Sagger missiles. Progress was made elsewhere in the offensive – the Akavish road was cleared, the 'marshalling yard' (a logistics area prepared before the war for an Israeli armoured crossing of the Suez Canal) secured and crossing forces were heading to the battlefront. Yet the continued resistance at the Tirtur–Lexicon crossroads meant that a huge log-jam of IDF traffic was forming back into the Sinai.

In an attempt to break the deadlock, at 0300hrs on 16 October, the 87th Armored Reconnaissance Battalion was committed to the assault on the crossroads, attacking from the west. Straight away, it was hit by tank, Sagger and RPG fire. The commander of the battalion, Major Yoav Brom, was killed when his M60A1 was hit, and one other tank was destroyed and two others damaged. It would take the rest of the morning for Reshef's units to secure the crossroads, at the cost of 60 tanks and 120 men. A key change in tactics was to hang back from the enemy positions but keep moving, firing on the anti-tank positions with HESH and (for the armour) HEAT rounds at long range, utilizing the M60A1's Add-On Stabilization kit to give accuracy for firing on the move. This approach weakened the defenders considerably.

By this point in the conflict the influence of the Sagger was still strong, but it was weakening. For a start, IDF tank crews were now actually becoming quite used to avoiding the missile – the 'shock of the new' had worn off. The benefits of experience are evident in this quotation from Yuval Neria, who fought throughout the Yom Kippur campaign:

> The sight of the Sagger was common to me by this point. I knew them from the first day. It has a balloon of flame like fireworks out the back, and it spins as it travels three or four meters from the ground. It makes a lot of noise and appears to be moving in slow motion. The Sagger is very frightening, but its slow movement gives me the feeling I can survive, I can avoid it, if I move only two or three meters with my tank at the appropriate time. The problem is, you have to move when it is two thirds of the distance to you. Then you don't give the man who sent it the opportunity to remaneuver the missile. (Quoted in Atwater 1991: 56)

One other issue for the Sagger teams during the fighting around Chinese Farm was that much of the action took place at close quarters – below the Sagger's minimum range – and (in later battles) with friendly and enemy armour intermingled, making for a complex range spectrum.

Against a backdrop of intense arguments about the development of Operation *Gazelle* (in essence, Sharon wanted to drive hard out of the bridgeheads already established on the west bank of the Suez Canal, whereas most other commanders wanted to consolidate the west bank before heading deeper into Africa), it was decided that Chinese Farm had to be suppressed decisively. On the morning of 17 October, ill-advised efforts by Egyptian armoured forces to sever the Israeli corridor to the Suez Canal resulted in a huge armoured battle in and around Chinese Farm and to the south and east of the Great Bitter Lake. Although losses were heavy on both sides, the Egyptians came off emphatically the worst – the 25th Armoured Brigade lost 85 of its 96 T-62 tanks. On the same day, the 14th Armoured Brigade, again with the 87th Armored Reconnaissance

Egyptian troops surrender en masse as the Arab campaign in the Sinai Desert and around the Suez Canal finally begins to unravel. The Israeli tank crews often did not have the resources or support to monitor the prisoners, which included Sagger teams and their weapons, so the soldiers were often left milling around until they could be secured by Israeli infantry units or they returned to their own lines. (AirSeaLand Photos/Cody Images)

Battalion in support, finally took Chinese Farm. Simon Dunstan, a historian of the Yom Kippur campaign, noted that 'The victorious Israelis were confronted with a sobering sight: highly organized infantry and anti-tank defences with great quantities of anti-tank weapons – guns and "Saggers" – lying abandoned' (Dunstan 2003: 84).

Both the 87th Armored Reconnaissance Battalion and the 600th Reserve Armored Brigade would continue to fight hard for several more days, this time on the western side of the Suez Canal, until the final ceasefire on 25 October. During that time, the M60 crews would continue to face the Sagger threat, and would lose tanks and tankers to them. For the 600th Reserve Armored Brigade in particular, there would be some grim fighting around Ismailia, with heavy losses. El Shazly, against the explicit orders of President Sadat and his seniors, had secretly withdrawn some forces from Sinai back over onto the west bank of the Suez Canal to reinforce the defence. These included much-needed Sagger units, which were concentrated around the bridges to prevent a crossing of the Ismailia Canal. One bridge, for example, was defended by eight Sagger launchers and six BRDMs with multiple Sagger rails. These ATGW forces, plus Egyptian artillery and infantry units, doggedly repelled several attacks by IDF armour and land forces. Sharon was unable to advance to Ismailia. In the end, however, the ceasefire and not combat decided the outcome of the war.

The action at Ismailia demonstrated how the Sagger remained a prevalent threat to the M60 tank until the very end of the war. Conversely, when faced by an aggressive enemy supported by fast-moving infantry and experienced in countering anti-tank weapons, Sagger teams found that their survivability dropped to a low level compared to the first days of the campaign. By the end of the war, many such teams had to decide whether to stay in the fight and die, or leave go of the Sagger joystick and flee or surrender, but at least live.

ANALYSIS

Assessing the strengths and weaknesses of both the Sagger and the Magach 6/6A is not just a case of quantifying and crunching data. The performance of these weapon systems, indeed any weapon system, is bound up with a bigger picture of tactical and human factors, plus the ebb and flow of the overall campaign. The typical position within most historical accounts of the Yom Kippur War (including this one), and from the personal memories of veterans, is that the Saggers were initially a game-changing presence in the Sinai Desert, but that by the end of the war the IDF had largely implemented countermeasures at least to limit the threat. Some analysts go even further, and question the efficacy of the Saggers in general. One such is former IDF armoured officer Lieutenant-Colonel David Eshel, whose analysis of the Sagger's performance in his book *Chariots of the Desert* is worth quoting at length:

> ... contrary to the general belief that the tank losses had been caused by Egyptian Sagger teams, more than half were actually achieved by enemy tanks firing from elevated ramps on the far side the Canal from ranges varying between 300–500 metres. The rest were lost to RPG rocket launchers fired from close range by tank-hunter teams hiding behind the Israeli-built ramps. Here engagements were at 50–150m. During the first stage [of the campaign], Saggers were launched mostly from the far side of the Canal, firing from protected positions on the ramps below the tank slots. From those vantage points, the Sagger crews could guide their missiles towards approaching Israeli tanks coming up the expected approaches which were well registered by the use of range cards. Sagger missiles require at least 300 metres after launch, to 'capture' them into the guiding optics which bring the missile on-target. In consequence, the most effective range for Sagger is usually not under 1000 metres. In this war, due to the shape of the terrain, such ranges were not genuinely available for the assaulting forces during the initial stage. Furthermore, most

During the Yom Kippur War, Israeli 155mm M50 self-propelled guns plus batteries of truck-mounted rockets bombard Egyptian positions on the west bank of the Suez Canal. The role of Israeli artillery is often sidelined in histories of the war, but it was actually vital in suppressing the Sagger threat. (AirSeaLand Photos/Cody Images)

of the immediate frontline was densely covered by smoke and dust from the artillery barrage, obstructing the visibility which is vital for the successful operation of wire-guided missiles ...

The introduction of the Sagger ATGM was no novelty to the IDF. There were previous encounters with that kind of weapon along the Canal during the late sixties, when Shmell missiles, an earlier version of the Sagger, were fired at Israeli tanks ... Although an extremely dangerous weapon, the Sagger was certainly not something the Israeli tank crews could not deal with, once they started operating correctly. Indeed, during the tank battles on 14 October, the Egyptian Sagger teams were almost totally ineffective, suffering severe casualties from Israeli tanks, infantry and especially mortars. Following the initial shock, which resulted in some serious crises, but was largely exaggerated by foreign correspondents (who gained their information largely from rumours circulating in the rear), the Sagger missiles almost disappeared from the battlefield, with the tanks gaining their former importance as a decisive weapon – a status they had actually never lost. (Eshel 1989: 142–43)

There are some important points made in this passage. Eshel attempts to demythologize the Sagger in this account, and rightly points out that we should not ascribe more significance to the Sagger than is warranted – Egyptian tanks, RPG-7 teams, artillery and minefields together played a larger role in the killing of Israeli

armour. It is also true that there was some exaggeration of the Sagger's effects by 'foreign correspondents' following the conflict; the Sagger was as new to them as it was to many IDF tank crews.

With due respect to his experience, however, Eshel makes some assertions that do not square entirely with the evidence, and into which we can bring some reflections upon the M60 and M60A1 tank. First, the optimal range for the Sagger was indeed about 1,000–2,000m, but that was an appreciable distance – many tanks rarely engaged enemy armour at more than that range. Indeed, the hit rate for a moving M60A1 at 1,500m with the Add-On Stabilization kit was about 75 per cent; going to double that distance would produce a majority chance of a miss. So, both the Sagger and the M60A1 were roughly in the same ballpark in terms of effective range. Regarding smoke and dust obscuration, these would indeed be a problem, but it was variable, often depending on the level of artillery employed. Film footage of some engagements shows Sagger teams firing in bright sunlight across open and expansive

The M60A1 loader had a critical role in putting down rapid fire on Sagger-team positions. His controls here are: (A) plunger (to release breech operating handle); (B) breech operating handle (opened the breech); (C) main-gun safety switch (allowed main gun to fire electrically when in the forward position); and (D) trip lever (allowed the safety switch to move from 'fire' to 'safe'). (US Army)

By the mid-point of the Yom
Kippur War, the standard IDF
response to the Sagger was
known as 'Sagger Watch'. In the
upper diagram, a unit of M60A1s,
accompanied by infantry in M113
APCs, advances towards Egyptian
defences, which are protected in
part by three Sagger teams. At a
range of 2,000m the Sagger
operators, working from slit
trenches set low in the
landscape, acquire their
armoured targets through their
periscope sights and launch their
missiles. An M60A1 tank
commander would have become
accustomed to spotting the
Sagger in flight from its flare
signature. At this range, he knows
that he has about 20 seconds in
which to respond. In the lower
diagram, the targeted M60A1s
undertake evasive manoeuvres,
such as making sharp, frequent
turns or steering the vehicles into
positions of cover, while firing
their main guns at the Sagger
operators' positions, each tank
putting down two or three HESH
rounds, while the coaxial machine
gun and the commander's
weapons (pintle-mounted
.30-calibre machine guns were
increasingly fitted to M60 turrets
during the war, specifically to
handle the ATGW threat) fire on
full-auto. If available, artillery and
also mortars drop rounds directly
down into the Sagger firing
positions. Here we can also see
one of the M113s moving to cover
and dismount its infantry, so they
can make a foot assault against
the Sagger operators. Through
this fire-heavy response,
therefore, the Israelis hope either
to kill the Sagger operators during
the 20-second missile flight, or at
least to force them to break away
from their joysticks and therefore
send the missile harmlessly into
the ground.

terrain. Furthermore, if we are going to claim that obscuration somehow reduced the effectiveness of the Sagger, we would surely also have to apply that argument to MBTs such as the M60A1, which relied squarely on the commander's naked vision and the gunner and driver's sight through periscopes and vision blocks.

Looking at Eshel's comments about the novelty of the Sagger, his statement that the IDF was already familiar with ATGWs is not borne out by some of the first-hand comments given earlier in this book, nor by the sheer difference of scale between isolated examples of ATGW fire before the war, and massive and systematic Sagger use during the conflict. Emanuel Sakal, another veteran of the 1973 war, quotes Gonen on this matter:

> Gonen insisted, 'The Egyptians concentrated fifty-four antitank missiles on every kilometer of the crossing. No tank could withstand that.' Facing this massive missile array was the IDF's thinly stretched tank alignment, which was incapable of providing an effective tactical answer and altering the battle framework.
>
> The tank units' biggest problem in the initial stage was their unawareness of the existence of the antitank missiles. In a briefing, before the October 8 counterattack, Lieutenant Colonel Haim Adini, commander of the 19th Battalion/460th Brigade, noted: 'No one mentioned that the Egyptian infantry had antitank missiles. So we had no idea what we were going up against.' Within a few days, impromptu combat drills and the addition of artillery, mortars, and the mechanized infantry's 0.50-caliber machine guns significantly reduced the number of tanks being hit by missiles, although they continued to plague Israeli armor until the end of the war. (Sakal 2014: 312–13)

Sakal's quotations from Gonen and Adini illustrate first that the Sagger anti-tank threat was emplaced in a density that had no tactical precedent, and secondly that many of the IDF armour crews (thinking about them specifically and not generically) had little or no experience with anti-tank missiles at all. Moreover, Sakal also puts some statistical meat on the bones of how effective the Saggers actually were, and here his analysis does draw a little closer to Eshel's:

> According to postwar debriefings of commanders and the Recovery and Maintenance Center's study of 214 damaged tanks in the two sectors, of all the tanks hit in Sinai, 41 percent were destroyed by hollow charges from tanks, antitank cannon, recoilless guns, RPGs, and Saggers. Twenty-six percent of the tanks were struck by Saggers, and 15 percent by other types of hollow charges. The Sagger undoubtedly had a significant physical and psychological impact on the armor force because of the tank crews' vulnerability, mainly in the first days; however, their effectiveness was disproportionate to the publicity they received. The mechanized infantry's lack of 0.50-caliber machine guns, mortars, artillery, tactical smoke for concealment and evasion, a war-fighting doctrine, and defensive drills all contributed to the antitank missiles' potency. (Sakal 2014: 312)

So, according to the data, roughly one-quarter of the IDF tanks destroyed in the Sinai were the result of Sagger hits. Taking on board Sakal's point about 'disproportionate publicity', the fact that one in four tank hits were attributed to

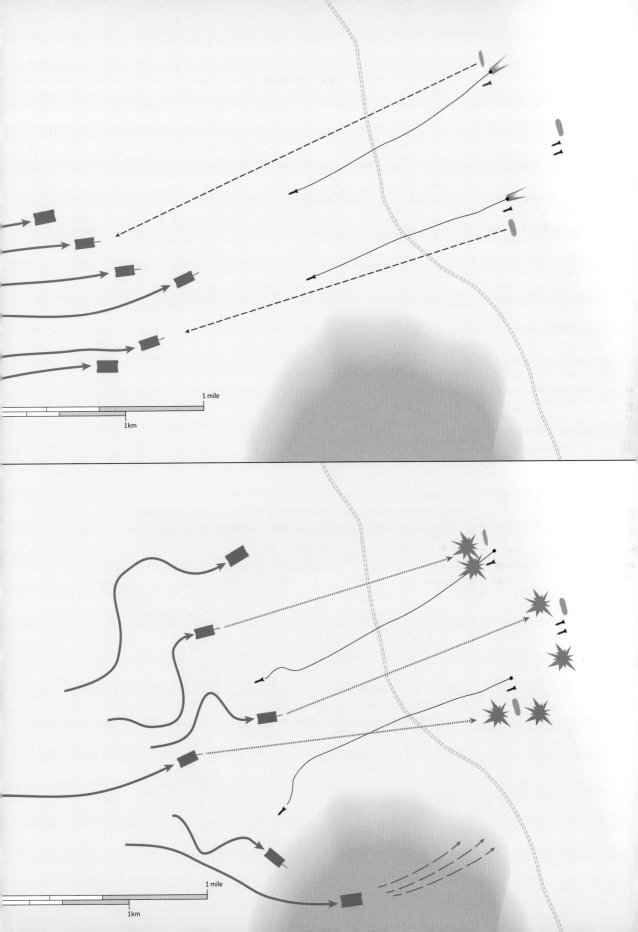

1 mile

1km

1 mile

1km

The heading of this TRADOC diagram says it all. It was quickly understood in the Yom Kippur War that the operator was the weak link in the weapon system. Future ATGWs would come to employ the 'fire-and-forget' principle, in which once the missile was launched, the operator did not need to guide the missile to target – the missile did that itself. (US TRADOC)

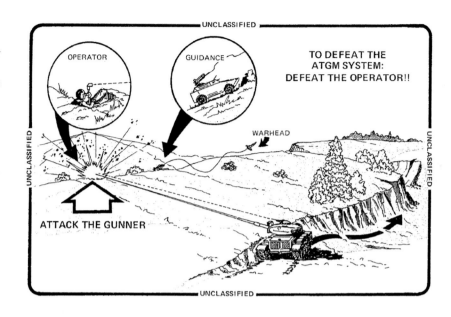

A US Army manual view looking up into the M19 commander's weapon station (CWS) cupola of the M60A1. The points indicated are: (A) elevation handle (for the .50-calibre machine gun); (B) machine-gun trigger switch; (C) .50-calibre machine-gun access door (for weapon loading or servicing). The IDF subsequently replaced many of the standard US cupolas with the Israeli Urdan low-profile version. (US Army)

Saggers is not insignificant. It must be acknowledged that the Sagger and M60 (to take our featured tank) are utterly disproportionate in terms of physical make-up, an anti-tank missile costing less than $10,000 being able to defeat a tank costing hundreds of thousands of dollars. Furthermore, no weapon is standalone decisive – in the same way that without the protection of infantry, MBTs are terribly vulnerable systems.

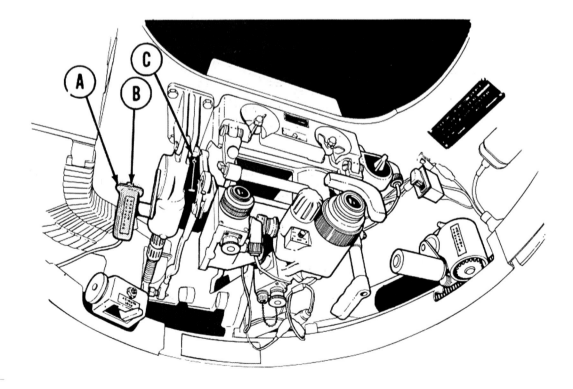

In essence, therefore, my argument is that the Sagger did have a serious, significant and lasting tactical effect on the battlefield, only lessened during the Yom Kippur War by the inevitable adoption of countermeasures that were developed on the basis of experience. Just as with the Sagger, however, lessons were learned about the M60 and M60A1. On the plus side, the new US tanks were reliable, had an excellent gun and accurate gunnery systems, a good supply of on-board ammunition and solid performance. The negatives were important. First, because of its turret cupola, the M60A1 had a high silhouette, making it easier for the Sagger operator to attack at range. (For this reason, M60/M60A1 crews quickly learned never to stay static within the 3km kill zone of the Sagger missile.) Second, the M60s gained a poor reputation for catching fire and burning easily when hit, not least by a Sagger. If not brought under control quickly, even a small fire could trigger ammunition detonation, and the sudden destruction of the entire tank.

So it is fairly safe to say that neither the Sagger nor the M60/M60A1 tank went into battle without tactical or technical issues. Then again, it is hard to find any weapon system or vehicle without chinks in its armour, literal or metaphorical. If those flaws are not terminal for either crew or weapon, and if they can be managed through sensible tactics, then the weapon will make a potentially significant contribution to battle, which both the Sagger and the M60 did.

About 40 per cent of the Israeli tanks damaged by enemy fire were eventually returned to the battlefield by IDF engineers, who worked tirelessly to keep tanks serviceable. Here, a crane is used to swap out the engine from an M60. The chevron on the turret indicates the 2nd Company, the company identification repeated in the shield on the fender. Note the HEAT shells laid on the hull. (AirSeaLand Photos/Cody Images)

AFTERMATH

On 25 October 1973, the final ceasefire resolutions issued by the United Nations brought the Yom Kippur War officially to an end, on both the Sinai and the Golan Heights fronts. Despite the brilliance of the opening Egyptian campaign, an Israeli recovery plus some poor strategic and tactical decisions on the part of the Egyptian high command had turned a potential victory, albeit a limited and realistic one, into a final crushing defeat. Once again, the IDF had demonstrated its capabilities to take on and defeat a far larger conventional army.

A sobering sight of IDF armour ripped apart during the fighting near Ismailia. The fact that the main tank in this image has had its turret blown off its mount indicates a catastrophic detonation of ammunition, resulting from either a tank-shell or an ATGW strike. (PD-Egypt)

Yet unlike the aftermath of the Six-Day War, there was no rejoicing among the Israeli military and political establishment. Although final Egyptian losses – 12,000 dead, 35,000 wounded, 1,000 tanks and 277 aircraft destroyed – were utterly disproportionate to those suffered by the Israelis, Israel was still cast into a long period of mourning. This small nation had suffered 2,687 dead, 7,251 wounded, and 400 tanks and at least 102 aircraft destroyed. Thus there followed a long period of often acrimonious soul-searching and political enquiry, most visibly embodied in the subsequent Agranat Commission investigation into the causes, course and failures of the intelligence services and the military.

The lessons were many, too many to list here, but they had a physical and tactical impact on both the M60 and the AT-3 Sagger. From 1975 the IDF began to purchase the new M60A1 RISE (Reliability Improvements for Selected Equipment) version of the tank, this featuring numerous

enhancements to its powerplant and engineering, plus the later M60A1 (RISE) (PASSIVE) tank, which had passive night-vision sights for gunner and commander and improved night vision for the driver. Indeed, such was the IDF's commitment to the M60 that it would go on purchasing updated versions (or upgrading existing tanks), including the M60A3 version introduced in the early 1980s, which had far more sophisticated gunnery arrangements, including an advanced M21 ballistic computer, and the removal of the commander's cupola.

In addition to purchasing US-made tanks, the IDF made its own modifications to the M60/Magach series following the 1973 war. To reduce the M60's silhouette, all existing and new tanks were fitted with the Urdan low-profile cupola. External machine guns were fitted as standard. Most important, the threat posed by ATGWs such as the Sagger resulted in M60s being fitted with kits of Explosive Reactive Armour (ERA), these essentially consisting of explosive panels that detonated outwards when hit by an enemy shell, the outgoing explosion counteracting the incoming explosive force. Through its modification programmes and purchases of the M60 series, the IDF has kept the M60 in service to this day, and it is still constantly engaged in a technological struggle against anti-tank missiles.

The Sagger has, if anything, enjoyed even greater commercial success, becoming history's most widely produced ATGW – a boost in image and sales followed the Yom Kippur War. From 1969 the 9M14P *Malyutka-P* (AT-3 'Sagger C') was introduced into Soviet and allied forces. This used a more advanced Semi-automatic Command to Line of Sight (SACLOS) system, in which the operator simply kept the periscope crosshairs on the target and the missile automatically flew to that point. It was a dramatic improvement over the previous guidance system, simplifying operation, reducing training times and improving accuracy. Since then, other nations have even produced radio-guided versions of the Sagger. Warheads have also received target-responsive updates, particularly during the 1990s with the introduction of improved HEAT (800mm penetration), dual HEAT (to cope with ERA), and thermobaric (enhanced anti-vehicle and anti-personnel effects) versions.

By incorporating the lessons of the Yom Kippur War and the many other conflicts that have followed in the Middle East and elsewhere, the M60 tank and the Sagger

A modern IDF M60A1 tank fitted with the Urdan low-profile cupola plus Blazer Explosive Reactive Armour (ERA) panels on the side of the turret, designed to counteract the inward penetration of a shaped charge through outward explosive force. Note also how additional external machine guns have been fitted to the turret. (Bukvoed/CC BY 2.5)

missile have remained relevant to the modern battlefield. At the time of writing, Saggers are regularly killing Syrian tanks during the brutal civil war in that country (although the US TOW (Tube-launched, Optically tracked, Wire-guided) ATGM appears to be the weapon of choice) and IDF M60s remain at readiness. It is not inconceivable that the IDF M60s and the Sagger will meet again in combat, as they did in the Lebanon in the 1980s, although we must always hope that they do not.

The Sagger threat has not entirely receded for the IDF and its tank crews. This Sagger, packed and ready in its suitcase launcher, was captured in 2006 during operations against Hezbollah in southern Lebanon. (AirSeaLand Photos/Cody Images)

BIBLIOGRAPHY

Asher, Dani (2009). *The Egyptian Strategy for the Yom Kippur War*. Jefferson, NC: MacFarland & Co.

Atwater, William, *et al.* (1991). *The Armoured Fist*. New York, NY: TimeLife.

Boyne, Walter J. (2002). *The Yom Kippur War, and the Airlift that Saved Israel*. New York, NY: Thomas Dunne Books.

Dunstan, Simon (2003). *The Yom Kippur War 1973 (2): The Sinai*. Campaign 126. Oxford: Osprey Publishing.

El Shazly, Lieutenant-General Saad (2003). *The Crossing of the Suez*. San Francisco, CA: American Mideast Research.

Eshel, David (1989). *Chariots of the Desert: The Story of the Israeli Armoured Corps*. London: Brassey's.

Gawrych, Dr George W. (1996). *The 1973 Arab-Israeli War: The Albatross of Decisive Victory*. Leavenworth Papers No. 21. Fort Leavenworth, KS: Combat Studies Institute, US Army Command and General Staff College.

Herzog, Chaim (2009). *The War of Atonement: The Inside Story of the Yom Kippur War*. Newbury: Casemate.

Katz, Samuel L. (1988). *Israeli Tank Battles: Yom Kippur to Lebanon*. London: Arms & Armour.

Kotras, Edward C. (September 1972). *Comparison Test of Tank, Combat, Full-Tracked, 105-mm Gun, M60A1 – Final Report*. Aberdeen, MD: Aberdeen Proving Ground.

Laffin, John (1982). *Arab Armies of the Middle East Wars 1948–73*. Men-at-Arms 128. London: Osprey Publishing.

Laffin, John (1982). *The Israeli Army in the Middle East Wars 1948–73*. Men-at-Arms 127. London: Osprey Publishing.

Lathrop, R. & McDonald, J. (2003). *M60 Main Battle Tank 1960–91*. New Vanguard 85. Oxford: Osprey Publishing.

Lee, R.G. *et al.* (1998). *Guided Weapons*. 3rd edition. London, Brassey's.

Logistic Management Division PMO M60 Tanks (May 1980). *M60A1, M60A1 RISE, and M60A1 RISE (PASSIVE) Series Tanks, Combat, Full-Tracked 105-mm Gun: Update System Assessment*. Warren, MI: Office of the Project Manager.

Nordeen, Lon & Isby, David (2010). *M60 vs T-62: Cold War Combatants 1956–92*. Duel 30. Oxford: Osprey Publishing.

Pivka, Otto von (1979). *Armies of the Middle East*. London: Book Club Associates.

Rabinovich, Abraham (2004). *The Yom Kippur War: The epic encounter that transformed the Middle East*. New York, NY: Random House.

Ramsey, Syed (2016). *Tools of War: History of Weapons in Modern Times*. New Delhi: Alpha Editions.

Sakal, Major-General Emanuel (2014). *Soldier in the Sinai: A General's Account of the Yom Kippur War*. Lexington, KY: University Press of Kentucky.

Tucker-Jones, Anthony (2013). *Images of War: Armoured Warfare in the Arab-Israeli Conflicts*. Barnsley: Pen & Sword.

US Army (July 1980). TM 9-2350-257-10-1, *Operator's Manual/Operator Controls and PMCs: Tank, Combat, Full-Tracked: 105-mm Gun, M60A1 (RISE); Tank, Combat, Full-Tracked: 105-mm Gun, M60A1 (RISE PASSIVE)*. Washington, DC: Headquarters, Department of the Army.

US Army Training and Doctrine Command/ TRADOC (February 1975). *TRADOC Bulletin 2 – Soviet ATGMs: Capabilities and Countermeasures*. Fort Monroe, VA: TRADOC.

INDEX